Fürst und Bolf

An Account of the Island of Mauritius

Fürst und Bolf

An Account of the Island of Mauritius

Inktank publishing, 2018

www.inktank-publishing.com

ISBN/EAN: 9783747780954

AN ACCOUNT

OF THE

ISLAND OF MAURITIUS,

AND ITS

Dependencies.

BY A LATE OFFICIAL RESIDENT.

LONDON:

PUBLISHED BY THE AUTHOR.

1842.

TO

THE RIGHT HONOURABLE

LORD STANLEY,

SECRETARY OF STATE FOR COLONIAL AFFAIRS,

&c. &c. &c.

THIS

ACCOUNT OF THE ISLAND OF MAURITIUS AND ITS DEPENDENCIES, COMPILED FROM THE BEST AUTHORITIES AND OBSERVATION, FROM THE DISCOVERY TO THE PRESENT PERIOD,

IS RESPECTFULLY DEDICATED

BY

HIS LORDSHIP'S

MOST OBEDIENT HUMBLE SERVANT,

THE AUTHOR.

LATE SUPERINTENDING SPECIAL MAGISTRATE, AND JUSTICE OF THE PEACE, FOR THE PLAINES WILHEMS, SECTION, OF PLAINES ; WILHEMS, AND MOKA, IN THE ISLAND OF MAURITIUS.

MY LORD,

Your Lordship having appointed me as a Special Magistrate for the Mauritius, I am indebted to that circumstance, for whatever knowledge or information I possess of the Colony ; and to you, therefore, I respectfully beg leave to dedicate this account of the Island and its dependencies. It is a well known fact, that of all the British possessions, less is known of the Mauritius generally, than of any other of our Colonies ; and when the vast National and Commercial consequence of the Island is considered, whether in reference to produce or her important position, in relation to our East India possessions and Trade, is a matter of surprize.

Should this brief account of the Island and its dependencies meet your Lordship's approval, and add towards the better knowledge of this interesting possession, my object will be attained.

I have the honour to be,

My Lord,

Your Lordship's most obedient,

And very humble servant,

THE AUTHOR.

To the Right Honourable the Lord Stanley,
Secretary for the Colonial Department.

CONTENTS.

CHAPTER I.

CHAPTER II.

CHAPTER III.

CHAPTER I.

The discovery and situation—The Dutch the first Settlers—The Dutch Admiral named the Island Mauritius—The Island taken possession of by the French—an Account of the French Settlers—The Island formally taken by the Chevalier Fougery for the French East India Company—An English Armament sent against it—Surrendered and Ceded to England.

THE Island was first discovered by the Portuguese navigator, Don Pedro Mascaregnas, in the year 1505. Mascaregnas gave the name of Cerné* to the Isle of France, supposed from the appellation of Cerné Ethiopia, given by Pliny to the island of Madagascar. The Dutch Admiral, Van Neck, was the first who landed on the island of Cerné, in 1595, when it proved to be uninhabited; Admiral James Cornelius, Van Neck's ship, was called the Mauritius, and he had under his command seven others, namely---the Amsterdam, Zealand, Gueldres, Utrecht, Fresland, and Øveryssel; they were separated in a violent storm off the Cape of Good Hope: five of them were driven towards the Island of Madagascar; they doubled the

* There is no reason to suppose that Pliny, or any of the ancient writers were acquainted with the Island; or that there had been any discovery of it, previous to that made by the Portuguese or of the other, now called Bourbon, and to which Mascaregnas gave his own name.

Cape St. Julien, and on the 17th of September, 1598, discovered the land which the Portuguese had denominated the Island Cerné. The Admiral sent two boats to reconnoitre the shore, one of which discovered the South East Port, sheltered from the winds, and appeared capable of containing many ships, with excellent anchorage. The seamen caught several large birds, which had suffered themselves to be taken by the hand; they discovered a stream of fresh water which flowed from the Mountains, and their report was, that the Island produced abundance of refreshments. The Admiral, however, not knowing that it was uninhabited, and not having time from the sickly state of his people, to make discoveries, ordered on the 26th, a large party to land and take such a station as would secure them from a sudden attack. On several succeeding days he ordered out boats to examine other parts of the Island, to discover whether it was inhabited.

They discovered on the shore about three hundred weight of wax, marked with characters; near the same spot they also saw a hanging stage, a capstan bar, and a large yard, the remains of some unfortunate vessel which had been buried in the waves.

They could not, however, find the least traces of human or quadruped inhabitants, after having ordered public thanks to be returned to God, for having conducted them to such a fair and secure harbour; the Admiral named the Island, Mauritius, being the name of his ship, also in honour of the Prince of Orange.

The Island is situated between 19°. 58″. and 20°. 32″. S. latitude and 57°. 17″. and 57°. 46″. East longitude, from 57 to 80 miles N.E. of the Isle de Bourbon, and 500 miles East of Madagascar. It is an irregular oval, length N. E. to S. W., about 36 miles; in breadth, varying from 17 to 18 miles, area, estimated at nearly 500,000 acres. The Dutch must be considered the first masters of the Mauritius, but there is no authentic reason to suppose that they really began to form settlements there until the year 1644. In the year 1648, Vander Mester was the Dutch governor of Mauritius: he is mentioned by the Abbe Rochon in a voyage to Madagascar, as follows:—

"Pionis, who had been commissioned to take possession of Madagascar, in the name of the King of France, was a man of inferior talents; he added to his other maliversations, that of selling to Vander Mester, then governor of Mauritius: the unfortunate Malagaches, who were in the service of the settlement—but it excited the Islanders to the highest pitch of indignation, when they found that among their slaves, there were sixteen women of the race of Loariths."

B

In the year 1712, the Dutch having possessed themselves of the Cape of Good Hope, and being anxious to put it into a state of defence, they by degrees transported thither all the troops they had at Mauritius, and entirely abandoned it. M. de Beauvilliers, Governor of the Isle of Bourbon after the Dutch had left, sent a party to take possession of the Island of Mauritius.

Although the French maintained a preponderance in both these Islands, their inhabitants for a long time consisted chiefly of adventurers of all nations, pirates, &c., many of whom, as the only means of enjoying connubial comforts, had married the negro women of Madagascar. In 1730, the Government, and also the East India Company of France, began to pay a serious attention to the Island, by sending engineers and other persons properly qualified to form a regular establishment. In 1721, the chevalier Fougery finding it advantageous for the French East India Company, took possession, fixed a pole in the ground forty feet in height, decorated with a white flag, and to which was attached the following inscription:—

VIVAT LUDOVICUS XV. REX GALLIARUM ET NOVARÆ IN ÆTERNUM VIVAT.

Hanc ipse insulam suis dictionibus voluit adjungi, illamqua jure vindicatim in posterum insulam francicam nuncupari. In gratiam honoremque tanti principis, istud vexillum niveum extulit Joannes Baptista Garnier de Fougery, Dux Navis Dictæ, le Triton ex Urbe San Maclovio oriundus, in minori Britannia, cum ipse huc appulerit, die 23 Septembris, eodem anno, in Galliam navigaturus, Des favente anchorus solirt."

Within a cannon shot of this place he set up a cross, on one side of whose transverse beam was inscribed, "Garnier de Fougery of St. Malo, C. the Triton;" with the Arms of France, and on the other side the following distich:—

Lilia fixa crusis capili mirire sacratæ ne stupeas; jubet hic Gallia stare crucem: Anno 1721.

After the possessions of France in India had all fallen into the hands of the English, the Mauritius continued to be of great importance to her as a naval station. It was estimated, that during the first ten years of the last war, the value of the British ships captured by privateers and other cruizers from the Mauritius, amounted to £2,500,000; at length a formidable armament being sent against it in 1810, it surrendered to our arms, and was definitively ceded to us in 1815.

CHAPTER II.

Appearance and general description of the Island—Soil—Difference of Climate on the Island—Herbage, or Pasture—The most remarkable Trees—Plants, Fruits, &c. &c.

THE Island appears bold and majestic, with mountains of every description and form, wild and irregular, as if rent by a violent effort of nature, presenting all that may be fancied of the effect of the "war of elements." The land runs rapidly from the coast to the interior, where it forms three chains of mountains, from 1,800 to 2,000 feet in height, intersecting the country in different directions, and from whatever quarter it is approached, the aspect is singularly abrupt and picturesque; there are many parts cleft into deep ravines, through which numerous rivulets find their way to the low grounds and terminate into several small rivers, by which the whole line of coast is well watered, from the foot of the mountains to the sea. The soil is in many parts exceedingly rich, consisting either of a black vegetable mould, or a bed of stiff clay, of considerable depth occasionally: the clay is found mixed with iron ore, and the débris of volcanic rock. The ground is covered with rocks of various sizes; in some places they appear in large masses, in others they are broken, but in such a manner, as if they had been separated and been united. The Mauritius are formed of them; these stones are of an iron grey colour, vitrify in the fire, and contain ferruginous matter. In the neighbourhood of Port Louis, and generally in the immediate vicinity of the sea, there is but a scanty cover of light soil over a rocky surface of coralline formation. The whole coast is surrounded by reefs of coral. There is no real sand, and that which is found on the sea shore, is formed of the madeporæ and shells, and calcines by fire. Its coast is lined with reefs, on which the sea breaks. According to calculation founded on geometrical measurement, its outline is ninety thousand six hundred and sixty-eight fathoms; its greatest diameter, which is nearly north and south, is thirty-one thousand eight hundred and ninety fathoms; and its greatest breadth, which is nearly east and west, is twenty-two thousand one hundred and twenty-four fathoms. Its figure is an irregular oval, and the surface contains four hundred, and thirty-two thousand six hundred and eighty acres. It has two very fine harbours: Port Louis, the capitol, on the western coast, and Grand, or, Great Port, on the eastern side of the Island.

There is a surprizing difference in climate in different situations; the windward side, or S. E. side, enjoying a lower temperature by several degrees than the leeward, (N. W.) owing to the cooling influence of the S. E. breeze, which prevails during the most part of the year. The Island produces three kinds of grass: along the sea shore there is a thick elastic turf, where herbage is fine, and the blade which grows to a sharp point, is sufficiently strong when dried, to pierce woollen cloth. In the hottest parts of the Island the pastures are composed of a kind of dog-grass, that runs along the ground, and shoots forth small branches from its stems—though it is very tough, the cattle is fond of it in its verdant state; but the best grass grows on the more moist parts, and the windward situations of the Island. It produces very large leaves, and is green and tender throughout the year. The greater part of the trees natural to this Island, have received their names from the arbitrary fancy of its inhabitants.

A large and very uncommon tree is found

among the rocks, whose substance is as soft as the turnip; it is called Mapou, or stinking wood, from its offensive odour, and is considered unwholesome. The Bois de ronde is small, hard, and twisted; when burning, it emits a lively flame—Bois de Cannelle. The cinnamon wood so called, from a slight resemblance to the real spice tree of that name, is among the largest of the Island: its wood is useful in joinery work, and resembles that of the walnut tree, both in colour and veins; when first worked up, it emits a fœtid smell—a peculiarity which it possesses in common with the flower of the cinnamon. Its seeds are enveloped in a red peel of a sour but very agreeable taste.

The Natte—there are two kinds: the one bearing a large, and the other a small leaf. The carpenter finds it a very useful wood.

Bois d' Olive, so called from a slight resemblance of its leaves, to those of the olive tree, furnishes very durable timber for building.

The Bois de Pomme is a red wood.

The Benjoin, so called from its compact quality, is admirably calculated for the purposes of the wheelwright. It is very thick, and never splits. The Colophane, which yields a resinous juice, is one of the largest trees in the Island.

Le Bois de lait. The milk wood, so called from its milky juice.

Le Bois puant. The stinking wood ; it emits an unpleasant odour, but is excellent. timber.

The Bois de Fougue is a large creaking tree, whose bark is very tough: it yields a milky juice, which the Blacks use medicinally ; but the most important of all, it being a very important article of commerce, is the Ebony Tree. Its bark is white, with a large stiff leaf, which is pallid beneath, and whose upper surface is verdant. Its heart alone is black, while its top is white. In a trunk of six inches square, there is not more than two inches of ebony. The odour of the wood in a fresh state is disagreeable in the extreme, but its flower throws forth the scent of the clove. It produces a fruit like the Medlar, full of a viscous juice, which is sweet and of an agreeable flavour. To enumerate the whole of the various trees, shrubs, and plants, which flourish here, and which has been brought at various periods from Madagascar, China; various parts of India, and the Cape of Good Hope, would be a work of itself. The banks of the streams which alternately wind in silence, or impetuously rush through the woods, are covered with trees, from whence are suspended bunches of the Scholopendriæ, and flowers of the creaking plants. The fallen trunks of trees are covered with enormous fungi, waved with different colours; there is also an infinite variety of Ferns, and the common moss of Sarohe is here seen, but of a much larger growth. Instead of the seeds which we are accustomed to see on the sides of the rivers, the Songes grow in abundance along these streams: they are a kind of nymphea, and resemble the water-lily, so great an ornament to our tranquil pools. The water-cress is found in the rivulets.

The Brette, whose name in the Indian language signifies an eatable leaf, is a species of morel: there are two kinds of them, the one called the Brette of Madagascar, whose leaf is somewhat thorny, but of a sweet taste, and a purgative quality; the other, which is in more common use, is served at table as spinach. It grows every where, and is much esteemed, both by the White, as well as the Black population.

The Manioc grows in the driest spots. It is a shrub, whose leaf resembles that of hemp: its root is as long, and frequently as thick, as a man's arm; and when grated, will make good cakes. It may be almost considered the daily food of the Blacks, and is also much

C

esteemed by the planters for their own tables. M. de la Bourdonnais procured it from the Island of Madeira. It quickly increases, and is a very nutritious substance; and it may be deemed one of the most valuable plants the Island produces. The Maize, or Indian corn, grows here in the highest perfection. The Anænas, or pine apples, grow most luxuriantly. Spinach, cresses, sorrel, parsley, fennel, lettuce, and endive, thrive. The Pomme de terre, (potatoe,) Solanum Americanum, or Cambar: its skin is blue like a violet, but white within; it multiplies considerably, and is preferable to the European chesnut. Mignionette, balsam, tuberose, larkspur, China aster, and small pinks—all flourish as in Europe; anemones, ranunculas, and the Indian rose, also the stock and poppy.

CHAPTER III.

The first Planters from the Island of Bourbon—M. de la Bourdonnais considered the first Founder of the Colony—Natives of Madagascar—The Landing of them—Conduct of a Master of a Vessel, as related by Admiral Kempenfelt.

The first Settlers, as before stated, consisted of adventurers of all nations, together with certain French planters from the Island of Bourbon; the latter brought with them simplicity of manners, good faith, and an hospitable disposition. When M. de la Bourdonnais, who may be considered the founder of the Colony, had rendered this Island by his judicious conduct interesting, persons of all conditions became Settlers; but the agents of the French East India Company possessed all the principal employments in the Island, much to the discouragement of the enterprizing Settlers. The whole of the public establishment was at their disposal; they controuled the civil power and police. Some of the agents cleared the land and built houses, all of which they disposed of at a very exorbitant price; from these, and other malpractices, there was consequently a great outcry against them, but complaint was of no avail, as the power was entirely in their own hands. To complete the settlement of this Island, some merchants, with small capitals, arrived, and employed themselves in forming petty monopolies; they soon became obnoxious, and acquired the name, Banians. Such was the situation of this Colony in the year 1765, when it was ceded to the King of France. The Black population consisted of the natives of the Island of Madagascar, and the Malabar coast; the latter came from Pondicherry, and let themselves out for a number of years: they are sober and economical.

The natives of Madagascar are good looking—some of them are only brown; the Balambous have long hair—some of them have fair hair. They are dexterous, intelligent, and have a sense of gratitude and honour. The linens, which the women weave, are very fine and well dyed; these they cast round them in a graceful manner, and the way in which they arrange their hair, produces a pleasing head-dress: it consists of curls and tresses, very tastefully blended together. They are passionately fond of dancing and music; their instrument is the Tantam, which is made of the Gourd, from whence they draw a soft harmonious sound, with which they accompany the airs they compose. Love is the general subject, and the girls dance to the songs of their lovers; the spectators beat time, and applaud. Such were their qualifications and manners, when they were brought to the Island in slavery. They were disembarked without clothing of any kind, but a strip of linen round their loins. The planters then examined them, and made their purchases accordingly, the men being placed on one side of the beach, and the women with their children on the other; brothers, sisters, friends, and lovers, were then separated, and led away to the respective plantations in paroxysms of despair to lead the following life:—

At day-break, the smacking of a whip was the signal to call them to work; they then proceeded to the plantation, where they laboured in a state of nakedness in the heat of the sun. For the least act of negligence, they were tied hand and foot to a ladder, when the overseer flogged them on the back with a long whip; to describe the severity with which these, and other horrid punishments were inflicted, would harrow the feelings; but the object is not to discuss the subject of slavery, on which there exists unfortunately a diversity of opinion.

I will record only one instance of fiendish conduct of a master of a vessel, as it is related by Admiral Kempenfelt. Speaking of the Island of Bourbon, he states, " that the inhabitants of the Island are subject to the same danger and desolation, as those of the Mauritius, from the runaway slaves who inhabit the woods; they were at a former period estimated at the number of a thousand, but in consequence of considerable rewards offered to those who should kill, or take them, they are now supposed to be reduced to two hundred; for each of them taken alive, or dead, the Company gives a well conditioned slave, who is generally valued at one hundred dollars. The captain of a ship, some time since, destroyed upwards of forty of them by the following stratagem;—As he knew that from the abodes in the summit of the mountains, they could perceive every thing that passed in the road where the vessel lay; he ordered some biscuit, cheese, and several bottles of brandy, with arsenic, to be put on board a canoe, and employed two of his sailors to take this treacherous cargo on shore, and to appear to enjoy the contents of it; nor was it long before the wretched people, who were the objects of this perfidious design, came down with the utmost precipitation to seize the booty; the sailors then regained their boat with some apparent reluctance, and the Blacks, who thought that they had possessed themselves of a very valuable prize, instantly began to gratify themselves in the consumption of it. On the following morning, twenty of them were found dead, and about the same number still living, who were so swelled from the quantity of water they had drunk at a neighbouring spring, that they were incapable of quitting the spot. On the following day, they all passed into the next world, where it is probable, they found a more happy allotment than the captain will experience, when he has made the same voyage."

The Madagascar Blacks are naturally of a lively disposition, but slavery changed them; love alone seemed to allay their painful feelings, for they would exert themselves to the utmost to obtain a wife, and if they could choose for themselves, they preferred the steady woman to the giddy girl; they immediately gave them all they possessed, and if their wives lived in another plantation, they would undertake the most difficult and dangerous journeys to see them, neither fearing fatigue or punishment. Parties of them would frequently meet to dance to the mournful sound of a Gourd filled with peas, in the middle of the night, beneath the shelter of a rock.

CHAPTER IV.

Description of Port Louis—The Mountains—Trade of the Port, with Australia, Bombay, Calcutta, Cape of Good Hope, British America, Bordeaux, Marseilles, and Malagascar—Public Revenue—The Alteration of the Duty upon Sugar, and its Effect—Exports of Sugar—Imports—Number of Ships, and the amount of Tonnage that entered the Port—Tides, &c.

PORT LOUIS, the Capitol and seat of government, is situated on the west side of the Island, in latitude 20° 9″, longitude, 57° 41″ east—population, 26,000; it is situated at the bottom of a triangular formed bay, the entrance to which is rather difficult. Strangers on first landing, are much amused by the variety of features, complexions, and attire, displayed in the town; for here you see Europeans, Chinese, Malays, Hindoos, Africans, and Arabs, mingling together; Blacks, (criminals,) chained in pairs, drawing carts, others perfectly naked, with the exception of a piece of cloth round the waist. The shops are rather gay in appearance than otherwise, and are fitted up in that neat and elegant style, peculiar to France. The streets are wide, clean, and airy; the best

D

are, the Rue de Rampart, and the Rue Marengo. The principal promenade, is the Champ de Mars, an exceeding good plain, extending gradually from the mountains, which has very much the appearance of an amphitheatre. Neat houses, in the cottage style, are built round the Champ de Mars, others are scattered along the various parts of the mountains, the whiteness of which, shown among the numerous trees in which they are embosomed, and the delightful view which they command, render these elevated houses very desirable. At the west extremity of the town, are some extensive and very commodious barracks—the town and harbour are strongly fortified ; the market is a very good one, and is generally well supplied. The mountains, at whose feet the town of Port Louis is separated, are the Pouce, so called from the point of the mountain terminating in a remarkable manner, having the resemblanee of the shape of a thumb ; the top of the mountain forms a level, which is steep on every side, and is not less than a league and a half in circumference, and is covered with wood. The most elevated mountain is called Peter Botte, and has a very remarkable and singular appearance, and from its peculiar form, was considered inaccessible, however, to the surprize of all acquainted with the mountain. Captain Lloyd, chief civil engineer, Lieutenant Phillpotts, of the 29th regiment, and Lieutenant Taylor, on the 7th September, 1833, accomplished the ascent, the particulars of which is worthy of perusal, as related by them, and which will be the subject of another chapter.

The hospital is situated a short distance from Port Louis on the rise of the hill on the other side of the grand river, and the commencement of the district of Plaines Wilhems. It is a very commodious building, and is in every respect well adapted for the unfortunate inmates.

The Government House commands a fine view of the sea and harbour, and is facing the landing place; adjoining the Governor's house, is the Colonial Secretary's, and other government offices, and nearly opposite, is the Custom House.

The Theatre is much better than the majority of our provincial houses.

There are subscription reading rooms, where strangers are admitted free, upon being introduced by a subscriber. The hotels are spacious, and quite in the continental style.

On the morne Découverte is a signal post, from which height vessels are seen at a considerable distance at sea, and are signalized, so that the merchants and others interested in the arrivals, are made acquainted, that certain vessels are off the Island, whether ships, brigs, or schooners, many hours before the ships can get into harbour. The Pouce, Peter Botte, Découverte mountains, separate Moka from. Port Louis.

In the hurricane months, the anchorage of Port Louis cannot be deemed safe. In Port Louis, may be seen frequently the vessels and flags of all nations and countries, with their produce. Australia has become a large consumer of the produce of the Mauritius. Vessels at Sydney, Van Dieman's Land, &c. are often advantageously employed in running across to the Island, and loading back, or to England with sugar. A good trade is carried on from Bombay to the Island in grain, and all description of India manufactures ; but Calcutta commands the leading feature of the trade in rice, wheat, and gram. The Cape of Good Hope supplies horses, mules, wheat, oats, barley, flour, beef, tongues, dried fish, and poultry ; in return, the syrup sugars are exported to the Cape, affording a field for speculation, and the advantageous employment of tonnage. British America supplies deals, fish, and flour, and in return takes sugar ; at present, the trade is chiefly with Halifax. Wines, of which the consumption is very great, is supplied from Bordeux and Marseilles. Madagascar largely supplies cattle, and also grain ; there are a number of vessels constantly employed in this trade belonging to the Port.

The public Revenue, in 1835, amounted to £187,780, and the internal Colonial expenditure, to £177,740, leaving a surplus about £10,000, which was to be paid over in aid of the expenditure incurred in Great Britain the same year, on account of the Colony. Parl. paper, No. 632 ; Sess. 1840.

The greater portion of the Revenue is derived from the customs duties received principally at Port Louis. Previously to 1825, the sugar, and other articles exported from the Mauritius into Great Britain, were charged with the same duties that were laid on such articles when imported from India ; but at the period now alluded to, the produce of the Mauritius was admitted into our markets at the same rate as the West India produce, which were then materially lower than those imposed on our eastern produce. This alteration of the duties gave a great stimulus to cultivation in the Mauritius, particularly to that of sugar, which has since been raised to the almost total exclusion of coffee, indigo, and cotton, that were previously produced in considerable quantities, the coffee especially being of an excellent quality ; next to sugar, black wood, or ebony, of which there is an immense supply, and tortoise shell, are the principal articles of export. The exports of sugar from the Mauritius, amounted in 1812, to less than one million of pounds. In 1814, they amounted to 1,034,294 lbs., and in 1818, to 7,908,380 lbs. since then ; but especially since the modification of the duties in 1825, there has been a most extraordinary increase in the export of sugar from the Island, it amounted in

1820 to 15,524,755 lbs.
1825 — 21,739,766 „
1826 — 42,489,416 „
1830 — 67,926,692 „
1835 — 64,854,515 „
1836 — 63,357,317 „
1837 — 68,478,874 „
11th Jan. 1842 — 46,022,400 „

but the export of other things are comparatively trifling, having amounted in 1836, to only 15,819 gallons of rum, or arrack, 23,358 lbs. cloves, and 664,369 of ebony. In 1837, the total value of the imports amounted to £1,035,783, of which cotton manufacturers, and other articles from Great Britain, made £345,744 ; the total value of the exports, including £77,792; for imports reimported during the same year, amounted to £831,050. The total export of sugar for that year, to Great Britain and the Cape of Good Hope, and some small quantities for other places, amounted to 68,478,874 ; among the imports were, 54,605,000 lbs. of rice, and nearly 5,000,000 of wheat from India, with considerable supplies from the Cape of Madagascar. During the same year, 433 British ships, of the aggregate burthen of 95,831 tons, and 65 foreign ships, of the burthen of 16,492 tons, entered the ports of the Island. The tides are not very perceptible ; the common tides, rise at most but two feet two inches. It is high water at noon, at the new and full moon. The winds have a considerable influence on the tides, for they are elevated by those of the west and north west.

The heat is greater at Port Louis than in any other part of the Island, as the mountains intercepts the South East wind, which prevails throughout the year.

CHAPTER V.

The Ascent of Captain Lloyd, Lieutenant Phillpotts, and Lieutenant Taylor, to the top of the Peter Botte Mountain.

The most extraordinary mountain in appearance, is that which bears the name of Peter Botte, from a person, who is said by tradition to have climbed to its summit many years ago, and to have lost his life in coming down again. The attempt has been several times made by our own countrymen since the Island became a British possession, but always till now, in vain. The exploit, however, has been at length accomplished. The account of its successful performance, is given in a letter from one of the parties in the enterprize, which was communicated to the Geographical Society by Mr. Barrow.

"From most points of view," says the writer, "the mountain seems to rise out of the range, which runs nearly parallel to that part of the sea coast, which forms the bay of Port Louis; but on arriving at its base, you find that it is actually separated from

E

the rest of the range, by a ravine or cleft of a tremendous depth ; it appears from the account, to be about eighteen hundred feet high. Captain Lloyd, chief civil engineer, accompanied by Mr. Dawkins, had made an attempt in 1831 to ascend the mountain, and had reached what is called the neck, where they planted a ladder, which did not, however, reach half way up the perpendicular face of the rock beyond ; still Captain Lloyd was convinced, that with proper preparation, the feat might be accomplished. Accordingly, on the morning of the 7th September, 1833, this gentleman, along with Lieutenant Phillpotts, of the 29th regiment, and Lieutenant Taylor, the writer of the letter, set out on the bold and perilous adventure.

" All our preparations being made," says the narrative, " we started, and a more picturesque line of march I have seldom seen. Our van was comprised of about fifteen or twenty Sepoys, in every variety of costume, together with a few Negroes carrying our food, dry clothes, &c. Our path lay up a very steep ravine, formed by the rains in the wet season, which, having loosened all the stones, made it any thing but pleasant ; those below were obliged to keep a bright look out for tumbling rocks, and one of them missed Keppel and myself by a miracle. Along this path, which was not a foot broad, they picked their way for about four hundred yards, the Negroes keeping their footing firm under their loads, by catching hold as they proceeded of the shrubs above them."

We must allow Lieutenant Taylor to continue the story in his own words.

"On rising to the shoulder a view burst upon us, which defies my descriptive powers. We stood on a little narrow ledge, or neck of land, about twenty yards in length. On the side which we mounted, we looked back into the deep-wooded gorge we had passed up ; while on the opposite of the neck, which was between six and seven feet broad, the precipice went sheer down fifteen hundred feet to the plain. One extremity of the neck was equally precipitous, and the other was bounded, by what to me was the most magnificent sight I ever saw. A narrow knife-like edge of rock broken here and there by precipitous faces, ran up in a conical form to about three hundred, or three hundred and fifty feet above us ; and on the very pinnacle, old Peter Botte frowned in all his glory. After a short rest, we proceeded to work. The ladder had been left by Lloyd and Dawkins last year. It was about twelve feet high, about half way up, a face of perpendicular rock. The foot, which rested on a ledge, with barely three inches on each side. A grapnell line had also been left last year, but was not used. A Negro of Lloyd's, clambered from the top of the ladder by the cleft in the face of the rock, not trusting his weight to the old and rotten line. He carried a small cord round his middle, and it was fearful to see the cool steady way in which he climbed, where a single loose stone, or false hold, must have sent him down into the abyss ; however, he fearlessly scrambled away, till at length we heard him halloo from under the neck, 'all right.' These Negroes use their feet exactly like monkeys, grasping with them every projection almost as firmly as with their hands. The line carried up he made fast above, and up it we all four shinned in succession. It was joking apart, awful work. In several places, the ridge ran to an edge not a foot broad, and I could, as I held on, half sitting, half kneeling across the ridge, have kicked my right shoe down to the plain on one side, and my left into the bottom of the ravine on the other. The only thing which surprised me, was my own steadiness and freedom from giddiness. I had been nervous in mounting the ravine in the morning, but gradually I got so excited and determined to succeed, that I could look down that dizzy height, without the smallest sensation of swimming in the head ; nevertheless, I held on uncommonly hard, and felt very well satisfied when I was safe under the neck—and a more extraordinary situation I never was in. The head, which is an enormous mass of rock, about thirty feet in height, overhangs its base many feet on every side. A ledge of tolerably level rock runs round three sides of the base, about six feet in width, bounded every where by the abrupt edge of the precipice, except in the neck, where it is joined by the ridge, up which we climbed ; in one spot the head, though overhanging its base several feet, reaches only perpendicularly over the edge of the precipice, and most fortunately it was at the very spot where we mounted. Here it was that we reckoned on getting up. A communication being established with the shoulder by a double line of ropes, we proceeded to get up the necessary materials, Lloyd's portable ladder, additional coils of rope, crowbars, &c. ; but now the question—and a puzzle too, was how to get the ladder up against the rock. Lloyd had prepared some iron arrows, with thongs, to fire over, and having got up a gun, he made a line fast round his body, which we all held on, and going over the edge of the precipice on the opposite side, he leant back against the line, and fired over the least projecting part; had the line broke, he would have fallen eighteen hundred feet. Twice this failed, and then he had recourse to a large stone with a lead line, which swung diagonally, and seemed to be a feasible plan; several times he made beautiful heaves, but the provoking line would not catch, and away went the stone far down below, till at length Æolus pleased, I suppose, with his perseverance, gave us a shift of wind for about a minute, and over went the stone, and was eagerly seized on the opposite side: 'Hurrah my lads!—steady's the word!' Three lengths of the ladder were put together on the ledge; a large line was attached to the one which was over the head, and carefully drawn up, and, finally, a two-inch rope, to the extremity of which we lashed the top of our ladder, then lowered it gently over the precipice, till it hung perpendicularly, and was steadied by two Negroes on the ridge below,—'All right, now hoist away!' and up went the ladder, till the foot came to the edge of our ledge, where it was lashed in firmly to the neck. We then hauled away on the guy to steady it, and made it fast; a line was passed over by the lead-line to hold on, and up went Lloyd, screeching and hallooing, and we all three scrambled after him. The Union Jack, and a boat-hook, were passed up, and Old England's flag waved freely and gallantly on the re-doubted Pėter Botte. No sooner was it seen flying, than the Undaunted frigate saluted in the harbour, and the guns of our saluting battery replied; for though our expedition had been kept secret till we started, it was made known the morning of our ascent, and all hands were on the look out, as we afterwards learned. We then got a bottle of wine to the top of the rock, christened it 'King William's Peak,' and drank his Majesty's health—hands round the Jack, and then—'Hip, hip, hip, hurrah!'

"I certainly never felt any thing like the excitement of that moment, even the Negroes down on the shoulder, took up our hurrahs, and we could hear far below the faint shouts of the astonished inhabitants of the plain. We were determined to do nothing by halves, and accordingly made preparations for sleeping under the neck, by hauling up blankets, pea jackets, brandy, cigars, &c., meanwhile, our dinner was preparing on the shoulder below ; and about 4, P. M., we descended our ticklish path, to partake of the portable soup, preserved salmon, &c. Our party was now increased by Dawkins and his cousin, a Lieutenant of the Talbot, to whom we had written, informing them of our hopes of success ; but their heads would not allow them to mount to the head or neck. After dinner, as it was getting dark, I screwed up my nerves, and climbed up to our queer little nest at the top, followed by Tom Keppel and a Negro, who carried some dry wood, and made a fire in a cleft under the rock. Lloyd and Phillpotts soon came up, and we began to arrange ourselves for the night, each taking a glass of brandy to begin with. I had on two pair of trowsers, a shooting waistcoat, jacket, and a huge flushing jacket over that, a thick woollen sailor's cap, and two blankets ; and each of us lighted a cigar as we seated ourselves, to wait for the appointed hour of our signal of success.

" It was a glorious sight to look down from that giddy pinnacle over the whole island, lying so calm and beautiful in the moonlight, except where the broad black shadows of the other mountains intercepted the light. Here and there we could see a light twinkling in the plains, over the fire of some sugar manufactory ; but not a sound of any sort reached us, except an occasional shout from the party down on the shoulder, (we four being the only ones above.) At length, in the direction of Port Louis, a bright flash was seen, and, after a long interval, the sullen boom of the evening gun. We then prepared our pre-arranged signal, and whiz went a rocket from our nest, lighting up for an instant the peaks of the hills below us, and then leaving us in darkness. We next burnt a blue light, and nothing can be conceived more perfectly beautiful than the broad glare against the overhanging rock. The wild-looking group we made in our uncouth habiliments, and the narrow ledge on which we stood, were all quite distinctly shown, while many of the tropical birds, frightened at our vagaries, glanced by in the light, and then swooped away, screeching, into the gloom below ; for the gorge below was dark as Erebus. We burnt another blue light, and threw

F

up two more rockets, when our laboratory being exhausted, the patient-looking, insulted moon, had it all her own way again. We now rolled ourselves up in our blankets, and having lashed Phillpotts, who is a determined sleep-walker, to Keppel's leg, we tried to sleep ; but it blew strong before the morning, and was very cold. We drank all our brandy, and kept tucking-in the blankets the whole night without success.

" At day-break, we rose, stiff, cold, and hungry ; and I shall conclude briefly by saying, that after about four or five hours hard work, we got a hole mined in the rock; and sunk the foot of our twelve-foot ladder deep into this, lashing a water barrel as a landmark at the top, and, above all, a long staff, with the Union Jack flying. We then in turn mounted to the top of the ladder, to take a last look at a view, such as we might never see again, and bidding adieu to the scene of our toil and triumph, descended the ladder to the neck, and casting off the guys and hauling lines, cut off all communication with the top."

I have only to add to this animated discription, that, more fortunate than Peter

Botte, Lieutenant Taylor, and his friends, effected their descent in perfect safety. The warm congratulations of their countrymen greeted them on their return, from what the reader will probably agree with the author, in regarding as one of the most brilliant enterprises of this sort, which have ever been recorded.

CHAPTER VI.

The Government, and Military.

THE Government is vested in a Governor, with a salary of £7,000 per annum, and a Colonial legislative council subordinate to the orders of the sovereign in council. The Governor is aided in his duties by an executive council, composed of the military officer second in command, the Colonial Secretary, and the Advocate General.

The legislative council is composed of 15 members, seven of whom hold no official appointments; justice is administered in a supreme court, and criminal court, with three judges, a petty court, from which there is no appeal, and such other courts as the Governor may see fit. Several provisions of the old French law continue in force.

The troops employed in the command, have consisted either of two complete, or the service companies of three regiments of the line, with one company of sappers and miners, and half a company of artillery. The service companies of two corps, with the head quarters of the artillery, sappers, and Miners, are generally at Port Louis ; those of the other corps are distributed between the different stations on the windward side of the Island, having their head quarters at Mahébourg.

CHAPTER VII.

*Customs Duties.—Import Duties—Entrepot, do.—
Export, do.—Port Charge.*

CUSTOMS DUTIES.

IMPORT DUTIES.

GRAIN of all sorts, ploughs, and harrows, steam and water engines, and other articles of machinery, calculated to diminish manual labour, and being of British manufacture, free of duty.

Salted meat, fish, duly certified to have been cured at the Cape of Good Hope, New South Wales, or Van Dieman's Land, free of duty.

All goods, the produce of the dependencies of the Mauritius, or of the Island of Madagascar, with the exception of ebony, if imported in British bottoms, are admitted free of duty.

Live stock of every kind.

Bullion, barley, and oats, being the surplus forage of cattle imported; hay and straw, fresh fruit and vegetables, whether imported in British or Foreign bottoms, free of duty. All other goods, the growth, produce, or manufacture of the United Kingdom, or of any British possession, if accompanied by the necessary certificate of origin, and imported in British bottoms, are subject to a duty of 6 per cent., ad valorem, except flour of such origin, and so imported, which is subject only to a duty of 1 per cent.

Foreign linens, silks, leather manufactures, clocks and watches, musical instruments, books, (such as are not prohibited to be imported into the United kingdom,) paper, and wine of all sorts may be imported in British bottoms, on payment of a duty of 30 per cent.

Foreign cottons, glass, soap, and manufactured tobacco, may be imported in British bottoms, on payment of a duty of 20 per cent.

Foreign turpentine, olives, olive oil, almonds, raisins, anchovies, fruit dried, or preserved in sugar or brandy, lentils, macaroni, vermicelli, marble, rough and worked; nuts of all kinds;

pickles, prints, paintings, flax, hemp, tow, tar, pitch, lozenges, sponges, iron, unwrought, pig do., honey, ochres, may be imported in Foreign, as well as British bottoms, on payment of a duty of 7 per cent.

Raw drugs are allowed to be introduced from a Foreign port by British vessels, on payment of a duty of 6 per cent.—but Foreign prepared medicines so introduced, are liable to a duty of 16 per cent. salted beef, pork, and hams, may be imported from Foreign places, in British bottoms, on payment of a duty of 12s. per Cwt.

Foreign flour imported in British bottoms, is subject to a duty of 5s. per barrel, unless it has been warehoused in the United Kindom, or at any British possession, and is imported hence direct, when it pays only a duty of 1 per cent.

Foreign wheat imported in a Foreign bottom is subject to a duty of 1s. per bushel.

Foreign wine, whether in cask or bottle, can be imported only in British bottoms.

Foreign wine in casks pays a duty of 7½ per cent. "ad valorem" and that in bottles an additional duty of 7d. per gallon, and 1s. per dozen bottles, except when bottled in the United Kingdom, and imported hence direct, when the bottles are admitted at a duty of 6 per Cent. Foreign spirits imported on British bottoms pays a duty of 1s. per gallon, and 6 per Cent. ad valorem, and if bottled, an additional duty of 20 per Cent. on the value of the bottles.

All other articles if foreign produce or manufacture, not enumerated as above, may be introduced in British bottoms, on payment of a duty of 15 per Cent. ad valorem.

Arms, ammunition, and gunpowder, dried and salted hides, ink, oil, hair or skins, and coffee, sugar, and hams are prohibited to be imported except from the United Kingdom, or from some British posession; counterfeit coin and books, such as are prohibited to be imported into the United Kingdom; foreign refined sugar are also prohibited to be imported; sugar, coffee, and rum, from foreign places, are admitted to be bonded for exportation only when imported in British bottoms.

Coffee, the produce of British possessions, within the limits of the East Inda Company's charter, may be imported in British bottoms on payment of a duty of 6 per

G

Cent., if accompanied by a certificate of origin.

ENTREPOT DUTIES.

On goods exported from the bond warehouse in British bottoms, 1s. per. cwt.

Goods which have been first placed in bond and afterwards entered from the warehouse for consumption, are subject to an entrepot duty, if coming from the westward, of 1 per Cent.; and if from the eastward of 1½ per Cent. over and above the ordinary consumption duties.

Export duties on sugar, 1s. per 100lbs., ebony, 1s. per 100lbs.; coffee, 4s. per 100lbs. tortoise-shell, 6s. per 100lbs; cotton, 7s. per 100lbs.; cloves, 10s. per 100lbs.; clove stalks, 3s. per 100lbs., and indigo 16s. per 100lbs. net French weight.

On gums 6 per Cent. ad valorem

Ploughs, harrows, steam and water engines, and other articles of machinery calculated to diminish manual labour, are also liable to an export duty of 6 per Cent. ad valorem.

All other goods may be exported, whether in British or foreign bottoms, free of duty.

Foreign ships of any nation at amity with

Great Britain, may export from Mauritius any description of goods or produce, " whether British or foreign," upon the same conditions as British vessels, to be carried either to their own, or any other foreign ceuntry.

PORT CHARGES.

Pilotage, in or out, 6s. per foot, according to the draft of water.

Anchorage, 9¾d. per ton.

Boats and warps, £3. in, and £3. out.

Port clearance, £1. 4s.

An additional 10 per Cent is levied on vessels under 350 tons register, and 15 per Cent. on those above 350 tons; to cover the expence of a dredging vessel.

CHAPTER VIII.

Currency—Weights and Measures.

Accounts are kept in current dollars, a nominal coin divides into 100 centimes, and equal to 4s. sterling. The coins current in the colony and which, together with British money, form the circulating medium, are —the Spanish Doubloon=66s. The Bengal Mohar=33s. 4d. The Bombay and Madras Mohar=28s. 9d. each. The Spanish, United States, Mexican, and South American Dollars =4s. 4d. each. The Austrian Dollar, and French 5 Franc piece=4s. each. The Sicca Rupee=2s. 1d. The Madras, Bombay, Arcot and Company's Rupee=1s. 11d. each, and the Coast Rupee=1s. 7d. There is also a copper coin called Merkee, the relative value of which is as follows, viz :—

1 Merkee= $\frac{3}{4}$d.

16 Do.=1s.

64 Do. or 100 Cents=1 Piastre=4s.

$6\frac{3}{4}$ Do. = 1 Livre = 5d.

$5\frac{1}{3}$ Do. or 25 Sous = 4d.

$10\frac{2}{3}$ Do. or 50 do. = 8d.

16 Do. or 75 do. = 1s.

Weights and measures.—The import duties are paid at the Custom House upon English weights and measures, but sales are effected according to the Old French Standard, viz.

110lbs. French = 108lbs. English.

7 Ells. do. = 9 English yards.

1 Velt. = 2 English Gallons, old measure.

CHAPTER IX.

Remarks on the Climate.—General State of the Weather throughout the the Year.—The South East and North Winds.—Lunar Rainbows.

In so far as regards temperature, rain, physical aspect, and diversity of climate, this island exibits a very striking resemblance to Jamaica, though being south of the line, the seasons are reversed; summer extending from October to April, and winter during the rest of the year; the principal rainy season is from the end of December to the begining of April, but showers are frequent at all times. Hurricanes are not of so frequent occurence as formerly, they principally occur however in January, February, and March; the climate does not act with any prejudicial influence on the health of the white population.

The general state of the weather throughout the year is as follows:—

January.—Rainy and warm. Storms, which are sometimes accompanied with thunder, though by no means violent, and as the tempestuous season approaches, all navigation is prevented; in April the Fields become green, and the whole landscape assumes a more cheerful appearance.

February. — Violent gales of wind, and hurricanes with thunder; these hurricanes, which, till the year 1789, were constant in this month, have since that time ceased, or nearly so, the inhabitants however are not wholly unprepared for them, having experienced severely the effects of the hurricanes, at this period, in two or three remarkable instances.

March.—The rains are less frequent, the winds always in the south-east, and the heat moderate.

April.—The season is fine and the grass begins to wither on the mountains.

May.—Westerly and north-west winds; the season dry; but in the low grounds and the interior parts of the island the air possesses an agreeable freshness.

June.—The winds are stationary at the south-east, from which point they seldom vary; the rain falls in small drops.

July.---Wind in the south-east, strong breezes during the day which subside at night, when it becomes calm; the rain falls in slight dropping showers, and the air is so cool, as occasionally to require warm clothing; in short it is now winter, if such an expression may be employed in a country where the trees never lose their leaves.

August.---It rains almost every day; the summits of the mountains are clad in cloudy vapours, which descend into the vallies, accompanied with gales of wind.

September.---The same weather and the same wind; it is now the time of harvest.

October.---The temperature of the air is somewhat warmer, though it is still fresh in the interior of the island. At the end of this month corn is sown, and in four months it is reaped; it is sown again in May, and is ripe in September, so that their are two harvests in the year.

November.---The heat is now very sensibly felt, the winds are variable, and are sometimes in the north-east. The rains are accompanied with storms.

December.---The heat increases. The sun is vertical, but the heat of the air is moderated by the rains, which destroy the rats, grasshoppers, ants, &c. in short the winds and rains produce the same beneficial effects which other climates receive from the cold and storms of the winter season.

There are four seasons in the island of Mauritius, the first beginning in May, and is accompanied with south-east winds; at this time the island is subject to squalls and rain. The rains are in general very beneficial to the corn, though they sometimes injure it. The second season begins in September or October, at which time the south-east winds are succeeded by the north-west. The sun now approaches the zenith of the island, warms the atmosphere, and causes the rains and winds, which generally begin in December, when the third season commences, which extends to March. The fourth season then takes its turn, and lasts no more than six weeks, this is the dry season. This division of the year more particularly relates to the general cultivation of the island than to any other circumstance, as, in fact there are but two seasons, that of the winds from south-east to south, and that of the winds from north-east to north. The two intermediate seasons are caused by the change in the air, which is a kind of monsoon blowing from south-east to north-east; the south-east winds are strong and violent, but they are not dangerous to shipping, as they never exceed a certain degree of force; on the contrary, the winds from the north-east to the north-west, are weak, and interrupted by calms; this is called the rainy, tempestuous, and hurricane season, and receives that denomination because while it lasts, no ships venture out to sea, and the voyage to the Indies can only be made by a long circuitous course. The south-east winds gives a certain freshness to the air, but while they blow every-thing ceases to vegetate, more particularly those parts which are exposed to them; hence it is that trees and fruit seldom attain any degree of growth, or perfection, in the district of Pamplemousse, which is almost entirely cleared of its wood; orange and lemon trees suffer the most from the south-east winds, as they require shelter; those indeed which grow in the woods are flourish-ing and lofty, while such as inhabit the plain are shrunk or mutilated. This wind is so obnoxious to vegetation, that trees bear no fruit on the side that is exposed to it, while the opposite parts yield a comparative abun-dance. The tamarind, which possesses a more hardy nature, braves the malignity of the wind, and would therefore form a protecting shelter for the tender fruit trees which are planted in gardens, but it is of such a slow growth in this island, as to be thought undeserving of any care or cultivation. The Dutch, at the Cape of Good Hope, shelter their fruit trees from this wind, by intersecting their gardens with thick planted lines, or hedges, of oak. In fact there is no prospect of forming such a protection for the fruit trees in this island, but after a long course of years, as the growth of trees there, is very slow. The bamboo has indeed been planted for this purpose, but its roots spread to such an extraordinary distance around it, as to be injurious to the very trees it might be intended to protect. The nights are generally very fine, particularly in the season of the north-east winds. At this period the sun rises with a serene aspect: at about 10 o'clock small clouds appear, and continue to accumulate without any menacing appearance; they occupy but a small space, while their motion is almost imperceptible. A few drops of water fall from them, a certain sign of the rain which follows, far the sky is almost immediately, and so insensibly overcast, that it is impossible to perceive from whence the clouds have proceeded; at the same time the rain increases in such a manner as to render it impracticable to see any object at the distance of an hundred yards. These rains continue about two hours, but fall only when the wind sets in from the sea: when these inundating showers cease, vapours arise from the sea, and are stopped by the mountains. On the contrary, during the season of the south-east winds, particularly in the evening, a small rain is seen to fall, though the sky appears without a cloud, and adorned with stars in full lustre. At the extremity of the harbour rainbows are also produced by the moon; the lunar rainbow is a phenomenon very seldom seen in our part of Europe.

CHAPTER X.

Marine Productions.—Native Animals.—The great Bat of Madagascar.—Turtles, &c.—Locusts.—The Altropos, or Tete de Mort Butter-fly—Carias or Ant.—Lizards.—Gourami.—Gold Fish.—Birds, &c.

THE vieille is a blackish fish, like a cod, both in shape and taste; it is sometimes poisonous, as well as several other kinds, which however are easily known; those who accidentally eat of them are seized with convulsions, which sometimes end in death. In the island of Roderique, it is stated, the fleet under Admiral Boscawen lost, by eating this fish, so many men, that it occasioned the expedition to fail against the isle of France.

It is supposed, that these fish acquire their poisonous quality by eating the madreporæ. The poisonous fish, however, may be known by the blackness of their teeth, or by throwing a piece of silver in the kettle in which they are boiling, which becomes black if they are impregnated with deleterious juices. It is however worthy of remark, as a singular circumstance, that this fish is never found to be unwholesome when caught to the windward of the island; this is a proof that the madreporæ does not communicate this poison, because the island is surrounded with banks of coral. Some attribute it to the fruit of some poisonous tree which falls into the sea; this opinion is no better founded than the former, since the island does not produce any fruit that could produce such a pernicious effect. There is a wood pigeon, whose flesh taken as food occasions convulsions, but it is a bird of passage, and as this fish is found in every part of these seas, this fatal quality may be acquired on the neighbouring coasts of Madagascar and Africa. In the number of these suspected fish are several of a whitish appearance, with a wide mouth and a large head, such as the captain, and the carranque; those which have rough palates are supposed not to be dangerous; the smaller the fish the less danger is apprehended in eating them. The mullet is plentiful. There are other fish, like our whiting, of red, yellow, and violet colour. There is also the parroquet fish, which is green, with a yellow head, and wide hooked beak, they swim in shoals, as the birds, from whom their name is derived, fly in flocks. The armed fish is small, and of a very whimsical shape, its head is like that of the pike, and bears on its back seven bony bristles, as long as its body, the prick of which is poisonous, they are united by a pellicle, that resembles the wing of a bat; it is marked from its mouth to its tail with brown and white stripes, like a zebra. There is the porcupine fish, bristled over with long prickles, and the polypus, which crawls in the swamps, with its seven claws armed with air holes; it changes its colour, spouts forth water, and endeavours to defend itself against any one who attempts to take it; these strange fish are found in the ledges and reefs of the rocks, and are seldom, if ever, applied as food. The poule d'eau, a kind of turbot, is the best fish of these seas, its fat is green. There are white rays, whose long tails are covered with sharp pointed bones, and others whose skin and flesh are black. Whales are often seen to windward of the island, particularly in the month of September.

The fresh water fish are better than ours, and many appear to be the same kind as those which are taken in the sea, among these, the best are the lubin, the mullet, the carp, and the capit, that lives in the torrents formed by rocks, to which it adheres by means of a concave membrane, also very large and delicate shrimps or prawns; the conger eels are very large. Along the sea shore are found a great variety of shell fish, among which may be classed a shapeless, soft, and membraneous mass, in the centre of which, is a flat bone somewhat bent. In this species the common order of things seems reversed, as the animal is without, and the shell within; there is all the varieties of snails, cockles, and oysters. The island is surrounded with the madreporæ, which are stony, in the form of plants and shrubs. It is no longer doubted that the madreporæ are the work of an infinite number of small animals, although they bear an exact resemblance to trees in their appearance, stem, branches and mass, and even by their flowers.

The great bat of Madagascar, so called by M. de Buffon, is about a foot in length from its posterior extremity to its beak, and its wings stretch to about four feet; it has large canine teeth, consisting of four in the upper, and as many in the lower jaw; its muzzle is black and sharp, its ears are large and bare, its talons are hooked, large, and compressed, it has no tail; these bats are different colours, some of a red colour, others brown and black, they resemble the common bat in their interior conformation, the shape of their wings, and the manner of spreading them, when they fly; when these animals repose, they cling to the tops of the highest trees, and hang with their heads downwards, at other times they fix themselves upon animals, and has been known on man himself; they feed indifferently on fruit, flesh, and insects, they are so fond of the juice of the palm tree, that they sometimes intoxicate themselves with it, so as to fall to the ground. Their horrid shrieks are heard during the night, in the woods, at the distance of two miles, but they retire at the approach of day. Nothing is safe from the ravages of these destructive creatures, they equally destroy the wild and domestic birds, whenever they have an opportunity, and they will sometimes attack the human kind, by seizing and tearing the visage. It is very probable, as M. de Buffon observes, that the ancients borrowed their idea of the harpies from these terrible animals.

The indians consider them as a palatable article of food, particularly in certain seasons of the year, when they are full of fat, and even some of the French people, both in this island, and Bourbon, have brought themselves, in this particular, to follow the indian example; the negroes, however, hold them in the greatest horror, and no consideration whatever could induce them to have any other concern with these noxious creatures, but to destroy them, for which purpose they employ uncommon dexterity. It has happened that persons has been attacked while asleep, and bled to death by them, as they are powerful and subtle bloodsuckers, so that it is really dangerous to slumber in the open air, or let them enter a house during night, but fortunately these disgusting creatures are now but seldom seen. Formerly there was great plenty of turtles on this coast, but at present they are very much diminished. There is a very singular amphibious animal found on the sea shore, named the Bernard l'Hermite (Cancer Bernhardus Linn), a kind of lobster, whose hinder part is without a shell, but nature has instinctively taught it to lodge that part in any empty shell it can find, they are seen running about in great numbers, each of them carrying its borrowed house, which, when incommodious from its being too small, it changes, as opportunity serves, for one that is more capacious. The most noxious insects of the island are the locusts, which are too well known from the injury which agriculture receives from them. There are several kinds of caterpillars, some of which, as that of the citronnica, are very large and beautiful. There is also a nocturnal butterfly, which bears on its corselet a death's head (the Attropos, or Téte de Mort.)

There is a kind of insect that resembles the ant in appearance, nor is it less sagacious in forming its abode. These creatures make a sad havoc amongst the trees and timber, whose wood they pulverize, and with the dust form arches of about an inch in breadth, over which they pass and repass; these insects, which are called carias, and are black, will sometimes overrun the whole timberwork of a house; they will make their way into trunks, and other pieces of furniture, in the course of a night. There is a small beautiful lizard, about four or five inches in length, with very lively eyes, which is to be found in the houses, it crawls upon the walls, and even along the glass of the windows, it feeds on flies and insects, for which it will lay in wait with extreme patience, it lays small round eggs, about the size of a pea, which are white spotted with yellow. Some of them are rendered so familiar that they will take sugar from the hand, they are very innocent, and as they destroy the insects, are considered as beneficial domestic associates. There is a lizard, which inhabits the woods, and is extremely beautiful, being of an azure colour, inclining to green, with crimson streaks on the back, which resemble Arabic characters. Foreign fish have been brought here; the gourami was brought from Batavia; it is a fresh water fish, and is esteemed to be the best in the Indies, in flavour it is smaller than salmon, but more delicate; here are also the gold fish from China, which lose their beauty as they increase in size. A bird has been brought from the Cape of Good Hope, which is extremely useful; the Dutch call it the gardener's friend; it is of a brown colour, and the size of a large sparrow, it feeds on worms and caterpillars, it not only eats them, but it also provides a store for future wants, by hanging them up on the bushes and hedges, and if deprived of its liberty, will contrive to suspend a portion of the meat which is given to it, on the wires of its cage.

The martin has multiplied very much in this island; it is a kind of Indian starling, with a yellow beak and claws; it scarcely differs from that of the European bird, but in its plumage, which is less spotted; it has the same warble, the same aptitude to articulate words, and the same actions; it counterfeits other birds, and settles on the backs of the cattle, but it is most remarkable for its greedy consumption of grasshoppers. They always go in pairs, and at sunset assemble on certain trees which they prefer; after a general warbling the whole go to rest. They are not eatable. There is a pretty tom-tit, whose wings are dotted, and also the cardinal, a splendid little bird, more tame than our robin, and whose head, neck and belly, at certain seasons of the year, are of a bright red, the rest of the plumage is a fine pearl colour. This bird originally came from Bengal. There are three kinds of patridges, they roost during the night on the trees, as in other hot countries.

CHAPTER XI.

Table of the Geographical Positions of the most remarkable points in the Island of Mauritius, with the Height of its Mountains above the Level of the Sea, according to Geometrical Operations.

	South Lat.	East Long.	Height above the sea in fathoms.
	° ′ ″	° ′ ″	
Summit of the Great Round Isle........	19.48.55	57.45. 6	165
Summit of the Peter Botte Mountain	20.11.21	57.30.48	420
Summit of the Pouce..................	20.11.40	57.29.25	416
Summit of the Mountain of the Corps de Garde	20.15.22	57.26.48	369
Summit of the Mountain Du Rampart....	20.18. 2	57.23 23	396
The Highest Point of the Three Mamelles	20.18.28	57.24.42	342
Summit of the Mountain of Bamboo	20.18.57	57.42.46	322
Summit of the Mountain of the Black River	20.20.40	57.20.13	283
Summit of the Mountain of Port Bourbon	20.21.29	57.41.14	249
Point of the Mountain of the Black River	20.24.18	57.22. 7	424
Summit of the Mountain de la Savanne..	20.27.50	57.27.30	355
South-east Point of the Island.........	20.27.50	57.16. 8	
Point of Cannoniers	19.59.50	57.30.49	
East Point of the Great Isle d'Ambre....	20. 2. 9	57.40.28	
Point of Flacq	20. 9.49	57.44. 5	

CHAPTER XII.

Pamplemousse.—Tombs of Paul and Virginia.—Wreck of the St. Geran.

THE following, written by Bernardin St. Pierre, is such a correct, as well as interesting description, that we cannot do better than to quote it:—

"On the eastern sids of the mountain which rises above Port Louis, and in a spot that bears the marks of former cultivation, are seen the ruins of two huts; they are situated near the centre of a circular valley, formed by stupendous rocks, and which opens only to the north; on the left rises the mountain called the Morne de la Découverte, from whence signals are displayed to the ships which approach the island, and at the foot of it is the town of Port Louis; on the right is the road which leads from Port Louis to Pamplemousse, and beyond it the church lifts its head, surrounded by its avenues of bamboo in the midst of a spacious plain, a forest then succeeds, which stretches on to the extremities of the island. This spot commands a view of the Bay du Tombeau; a little to the right is Cape Malheureux, and beyond is the expanded ocean, on the surface of which appear several uninhabited islands, and among the rest the Coin de Mire, which resembles a bastion in the midst of the waves.

"At the entrance of the valley which displays a view of so many various objects, the echoes of the mountains incessantly repeat the hollow noise of the winds which agitate the neighbouring forests, and the hoarse murmur of the waves that break over the distant reefs; but near the ruined huts all is calm and still, and the objects which there meet the eye are rude steep rocks, that rise like a surrounding rampart; knots of trees grow at their base, in their rifted sides, and in their majestic summits, where the clouds seem to repose. The showers which their sold pinnacles attract, illuminate the dusky declivities with the colours of the rainbow, and feed the springs at their feet, which swell into the river of the Lataniers.

"In this seclusion reigns the most profound silence, the water, the air, in short, every element is at peace, the echo scarce repeats the whispers of the palm trees, the points of whose broad leaves wave gently in the wind; a soft light beams on the bottom of this valley, which the sun does not reach till noon, but his earliest rays gild the summits of the rocks, whose sharp peaks, rising above the shadows of the mountains, are clothed in tints of gold and purple, gleaming on the azure sky."

To this part of Pamplemousse, strangers are generally attracted on their arrival, it being the place which St. Pierre has so celebrated in his interesting tale of Paul and Virginia, and in which he has so beautifully and glowingly described it; in this spot is shown, what are represented to be the tombs of the amiable but unfortunate Creoles, whose mutual affection, and unhappy fates, few readers can peruse without emotion. On arrival, you find a pretty garden, with a walk bordered with rose trees, a streamlet of the clearest water running on each side, at the end of this walk you will perceive a red glaring monument, which you are informed is the tomb of Virginia; at the end of a similar path, on the opposite side, appears another monument, resembling the first, which

K

the enquirer is told is the tomb of Paul—imagination may then depict the shades of the ill-fated lovers, hovering about the spot they once so much delighted in, and where their remains repose—the mind softened with some such ideas, and pleased with having seen those celebrated tombs erected to the memory of the faithful lovers, who were separated in life, but in death united, and after all this sympathy, he learns at last, that he has been under a delusion, that no Virginia was there interred, and a matter of doubt whether there ever existed such a person as Paul. What flights of romantic fancy, inspired by the remembrance of the tale, are doomed to vanish when the truth is known! the fact is, that these tombs have been built to gratify the curiosity of the numerous visitors, eager to behold such interesting mementoes: formerly only one was erected, but there was so much enquiry about Paul's burial-place, that the proprietor determined to have another building as the mausoleum of Paul. These so called tombs, are scribbled over by the various persons who have been gratified with a sight of them, combining verse, sentimental remarks, and pathetic ejaculations. It is a well-known fact, that there was a young lady sent from the island to France, for education, during the time that M. de la Bourdonnais was governor, and that her name was Virginia, and that she was lost in the St. Geran. The wreck of the St. Geran occurred on the 24th of December, 1744. All the circumstances attending the loss of the vessel are recorded, and well authenticated, and the author has been assured by the sons of many of the spectators of that awful wreck, that their parents invariably admitted that the description of it was faithfully and correctly given, in every respect, by Bernardin St. Pierre, the particulars of which are so interesting, we shall make no apology in giving it in the words of that admired author.

" The heat was suffocating, and the moon, which had risen, was encompassed by three large black circles; a dismal darkness shrouded the sky, but the frequent flakes of lightning discovered long chains of thick gloomy clouds rolling with great rapidity from the ocean, though we felt not a breath of wind from the land; as we walked along we thought that we heard peals of thunder, but after listening more attentively, we found they were the sound of distant cannon, repeated by the echoes. These sounds, joined to the tempestuous aspect of the heavens, made me shudder, and I had little doubt that they were signals of distress from a ship in danger; in half an hour the firing ceased, and I felt the silence more appalling than the dismal sound which had preceeded. We hastened on without uttering a word, or daring to communicate our apprehensions ; at midnight we arrived on the sea shore, the billows broke against the beach with an horrible noise, covering the rocks and the strand with their white and dazzling foam, blended with sparks of fire ; by their phosphoric gleams we distinguished, dark as it was, the canoes of the fishermen, which they had drawn far on the sand ; near the shore, at the entrance of a wood, we saw a fire, round which several of the inhabitants were assembled, thither we repaired, in order to repose ourselves until the morning. One of the circle related that in the afternoon he had seen a vessel driven towards the island by the currents, that the night had obscured it from his view, and that two hours after sunset he had heard the firing of guns, as signals of distress, but the sea being so tempestuous, no boat could venture out, that a short time after, he thought he perceived the glimmering of the watch lights on board the ship, which he feared, by its having approached so near the coast, had steered between the mainland and the small Isle d'Ambre, mistaking it for the Coin de Mere, near which the vessels pass in order to gain Port Louis, and if that were so, the ship he apprehended was in great danger; another islander then informed us that he had frequently crossed the channel which separates the Isle d'Ambre from the coast, and as he had sounded it he knew the anchorage was good, and that the ship would there be in as great security as if it were in the harbour. A third islander declared it was impossible for the ship to enter the channel, which was scarcely navigable for a boat; he asserted that he had seen the vessel at anchor beyond the Isle d'Ambre, so that if the wind sprung up in the morning, it could either put to sea or gain the harbour. At break of day the weather was too hazy to admit of our distinguishing any object at sea, which was covered with a fog; all that we could descry was a dark cloud, which, we were informed was the Isle d'Ambre, at the distance of a quarter of a league from the coast; we could only discern on this gloomy morning the point of the beach where we stood, and the peaks of some mountains in the interior part of the island, rising occasionally from amidst the clouds which hung round them. At seven in the morning we heard the drums beat in the woods, and soon after the governor, M. de la Bourdonnais appeared on horseback, followed by a detachment of soldiers, armed with muskets, and a great number of islanders and blacks. He ranged the soldiers upon the beach, and ordered them to make a general discharge, which was no sooner done than we perceived a glimmering light upon the water, that was instantly succeeded by the report of a gun, we therefore judged that the ship was at no great distance, and hastened towards that part where we had seen the light. We had discerned through the fog the hull and tackling of a large ship, and notwithstanding the noise of the waves, we were near enough to hear the whistle of the boatswain, and the shouts of the marines; as soon as the St. Geran perceived that we were near enough to give her assistance, she continued to fire guns successively every three minutes. M. de la Bourdonnais caused great fires to be lighted at certain distances upon the strand, and sent to all the inhabitants of that neighbourhood, in search of provisions, planks, cables, and empty barrels. A crowd of people soon arrived, accompanied by their negroes, loaded with provisions and rigging. One of the oldest planters at this time informed the governor that they heard, during the whole of the night, hoarse noises on the mountain and forests, that the leaves of the trees were shaken, though there was no wind, and that the sea birds sought refuge on the land, all of which he considered as certain signs of an approachiug hurricane, everything indeed seemed to denote its speedy arrival. The centre of the clouds in the zenith was of a dismal black, while their skirts were fringed with a copper hue; the air resounded with the cry of the frigate bird, and a multitude of sea fowl, who notwithstanding the obscurity of the atmosphere, hastened from all points of the horizon to seek for shelter in the island; towards nine in the morning we heard, on the side of the ocean, the most terrific noises, as if torrents of water, accompanied by thunder, were rolling down the steeps of the mountains; a general exclamation followed, of 'there is the hurricane,' and, in one moment, a frightful whirlwind scattered the fog which had covered the Isle d'Ambre and its channel;

the St. Geran then presented itself to our view, her gallery crowded with people, her yards and maintopmast laid upon the deck, her flag shivered, with four cables at her head, and one by which she was held at the stern; she had anchored between the Isle d'Ambre and the mainland, within that chain of breakers which encircles the island, and must have been driven over a bar that no vessel had ever passed before; she presented her head to the waves which rolled from the open sea, and as each billow rushed into the straits, the ship heaved in such a manner, that her keel was in the air, while at the same moment, her stern plunging into the water, disappeared altogether, as if it were swallowed up by the billows; in this position, driven by the winds and waves towards the shore, it was equally impossible to return by the passage through which she had made her way, or by cutting her cables to throw herself upon the beach, from which she was separated by sand banks, mingled with breakers. Every billow which broke upon the coast, advanced roaring to the bottom of the bay, and threw planks fifty feet upon the land, then rushing back, laid bare its sandy bed, from which it rolled immense stones with an hoarse and dismal noise; the sea, swelled by the violence of the wind, rose higher every moment, and the channel between this island and the Isle d'Ambre was one sheet of white foam, with yawning chasms of black deep billows; the foam boiling in the gulph was more than six feet in height, and the winds which swept its surface, bore it over the steep coast more than half a league upon the land. The innumerable white flakes, driven horizontally as far as the foot of the mountain, appeared like snow issuing from the ocean, which was now confounded with the sky; thick clouds of an horrible form, swept along the zenith with the swiftness of birds, while others appeared motionless as rocks; not a spot of azure could be discerned in the firmament, only a pale yellow gleam displayed the view of earth, sea, and skies. From the violent efforts of the ship, what we dreaded happened; the cables at the head of the vessel were torn away, it was then held only by one anchor, and was instantly dashed upon the rocks, at the distance of half a cable's length from the shore—a general cry of horror issued from the spectators—sometimes the sea, in its irregular movements, had left the vessel almost dry, so that any one might have walked around it, but suddenly the waves advancing with renovating fury, shrouded it beneath mountains of water, which then lifted it upright on its keel. At last every part of it yawned asunder from the violent strokes of the billows, and the crew in despair threw themselves into the sea, of these seven alone escaped, and the unfortunate Virginia was one of the victims—such was this scene of horror."

As a confirmation of the above awful occurrence, annexed is a copy of a letter from Baron Grant, to a friend, wherein he alludes to the loss of the St. Geran.

"Isle of France, 28th December, 1744.

"It is now a year since we expected a large vessel, called the St. Geran, which was expected to bring the necessary supplies to these islands, and it only has arrived to be shipwrecked on this coast, off a small adjoining uninhabited island, called the Isle d'Ambre. The pilot, who had never been employed but in very small vessels, knew not how to guide so large a ship on this perilous coast, so that she was lost with all her cargo, and only seven of her crew escaped.

"We are destined to remain without those comforts and supplies with which this unfortunate vessel was laden, until the company, on being informed of the loss we have sustained, can make the necessary preparation to despatch another cargo for our relief; since this unpropitious event, some small vessels have arrived, which, however, brought us little more than accounts of the state of public affairs; the last of them indeed gave us the satisfactory intelligence, that the company had despatched several vessels laden with everything necessary for the welfare of the island; but, if they should delay their arrival, we must be content to go barefoot, like the negroes, and to clothe ourselves in the skins of deer, though that animal, which furnishes us with such excellent meat, begins to be less common than formerly in the forests, nor do the goats increase, whom I sometimes follow into their most difficult recesses. We must however be content to stay at home at present, as the few handicraftsmen we had, are departed for the war in India, &c.

(Signed) GRANT."

CHAPTER XIII.

Account of the Island as given by M. le Gentil.—Climate.—Soil.—Manioc. Crops.—Coffee Plant.

THE following account of the Isle of France has been given by M. le Gentil :—There are, properly speaking, no diseases in the Isle of France, that is to say, in the Plantations, for at the north west port the scurvy sometimes makes its appearance ; the south-east, on the contrary, is very wholesome, and persons afflicted with scorbutic complaints are sent there in order to be cured. The inhabitants, however, prefer the small and less healthy, to the other, which is one of the finest harbours in the world. The Isle of France may therefore be considered as a very happy climate.

The lands in the Isle of France bear a larger proportion of annual produce than those of France; they do not however lay fallow, nor are they manured, they appear very dry, poor, and acrid, and the vegetables draw all the nourishment from the water and the air, in fact, with a certain quantity of water, and proportion of heat, the most sandy soil will become productive, which is proved by those small rocky islands, scattered through the seas of the torrid zone, and covered with trees of the brightest verdure. The land of the Isle of France is of a dark red, and mixed with ferruginous matter. The sand of the ravines and rivers is the sand of a mine, that of the sea is calcareous, and in the year 1770, the governor, who had been persuaded by a private person then inhabiting the island, that he would produce crystal glass equal to that of France, some advances were made towards such a manufacture; the object of such a branch of commerce would be to supply the Indies. The manioc flourishes in the Isle of France, and the finest grow at Pamplemousses, and the long mountain; it remains eighteen months in the ground before it is fit for use. The maize is very successful; it requires a considerable quantity of water and heat, so that the season of the north-east wind agrees with it best. The district of Flacq, which is a quarry of rocks, produces the finest; such a soil is not favorable for corn, the inhabitants therefore clear away the smallest stones, and plant maize in the places they occupied, where it is found to luxuriate and grow to the height of eight to ten feet; though it generally requires a large portion of moisture, any quantity of rain is not necessary to it in this quarter, as the dews are very abundant, and and rocks, which keep the earth from becoming dry, preserve the soil in the requisite state of humidity, so that the crops never fail, and, unpromising as the soil is, the inhabitants look for two and sometimes three harvests in the course of the year—such is their wealth and their commerce. A certain portion of it they pour into public magazines, with the rest they nourish their slaves, barter for corn, and feed the hogs and poultry with which they traffic. They have every convenience that is to be derived from water, as Flacq is a kind of archipelago, on account of the various branches of water that intersect it; this quarter also possesses, in the low grounds towards the sea, some parcels of ground which is proper for the cultivation of rice; and M. le Gentil adds, that in his time it was that part of the island, which supplied the Company's magazine with such a necessary article. The plantations which are more exposed, and have none of these rocks, do not succeed so well in the growth of maize. I saw, continues M. le Gentil, on my return from Pondicherry in the year 1770, in the Isle of France, under the cultivation of the curate of Pamplemousses, a small corn-field, which wore a fine appearance, was of an equal height, of about three feet, and according to the declaration of the ecclesiastic, had in a former year yielded fifteen-fold. At Flacq the corn generally produces twenty-fold, and sometimes thirty, in fresh ground, but no more than ten in that which has been in a long and successive state of tillage, but to insure such a produce there must be a concurrence of favourable circumstances, the rats and the birds must be checked in their devastations, the rain must fall in that degree of moderation, as not to beat down the crop, and it must be preserved from the mildew. The small quantity of corn which is grown in the Isle of France, appears at first to be rather extraordinary, as the mode of cultivation is superior to that of Europe. There, it is sown, and here, it is actually planted, on account of the rocks, which will not allow the use of the plough, and more hands are consequently necessary, but the land is never relieved by a fallow, or sustained by manure. M. de la Bourdonnais, whose views in settling in the Isle of France were purely commercial, wished to introduce silk-worms and indigo. It is probable that cotton was brought into this island by that distinguished person. I have met with people, continues M. le Gentil, who have pretended that the iron of this island is of no value, but I differ in opinion from them, as I have samples of it which justify my dissent. It cannot indeed be denied, that it has a very moderate sale in the Indies, when compared with that which is exported from France, but that proves nothing more than the inferiority to European iron, without confirming the depreciating opinion of it; besides, the mode of extracting the metal from the earth, and the subsequent process to purify and render it malleable, must in a great measure influence its final value; the following experiment, however, will determine the qualities and nature of the iron found in this island. The masts of vessels, being made in Europe of a light wood, the circles of iron, which are applied to strengthen and support them, sink into it; in the Isle of France, the wood which is employed to splice the masts, is extremely hard, and not only resists, but, from its elasticity breaks the circles of European iron; those made of the iron of the Isle of France, employed in the French vessels during the last war, and worked by the forges of M. Herman, were the only hoops of this kind that resisted and remained firm, this circumstance appears to be decisive in favour of the iron of this island. It has been said, and many have believed it, that the whole of this island is iron. There is certainly some iron there, but not equally abundant, and the forges have been erected where the ore is the least prevalent. It is by washing the earth that the mineral is obtained, and some time since, it was brought to the gate of the kiln on the side of which the Patouillard is established, in a fine plain. These works were for some time successful, from the advantage of a favourable vein, but they have since been abandoned, though the place has not been raked. A small portion of mineral was however found in 1770, and that was fetched from more than the distance of half a league from the kiln, besides the mineral was poor, which was found in veins or furrows of little length, and but few feet under ground. The mine at Pamplemousses, if it deserves that title. is not rich, and seems to be furnished with what mineral it contains by the force of the rains, which

M

wash it down from the highlands into the plains. It has been said that one hundred weight of this mineral will give fifteen pounds of wrought iron, but M. le Gentil saw that nine thousand pounds of mineral, gave from fifteen hundred to two thousand two hundred pounds of cast iron; this is about twenty per cent, but then, fifteen hundred, or two thousand two hundred pounds of cast iron did not give half that quantity of wrought iron, consequently this mine did not produce more than ten pounds of wrought iron for each hundred of mineral. At Villebagne, the mine appeared to be more abundant, but it is at the distance of a league from the forges, in very elevated spots, and intersected by ravines and precipices; in the still more elevated spots, such as the military quarter of Nouvelle Découverte, the mines appeared equally productive, but, if Villebagne is excepted, these spots give but little encouragement to establish forges, as there is not sufficient water to answer all their demands, nor is it probable that the proprietors of the forges will ever go two or three leagues from Pamplemousses, among frightful mountains, and where there are no roads, to rake up the ground, in order to bring iron to their furnaces, besides these mines are, as it were, on the surface of the earth.

The French East India Company had set apart for these forges an extent of wood of ten thousand acres, called the Reserves, they then imagined that by making regular falls in these lofty woods, they would shoot forth again the following year, and that the young trees, being left untouched, would replace the large ones; but how many generations will pass away before this fine forest is reproduced? as, according to the opinion of M. le Gentil, the trees once cut down in the Isle of France, do not grow again; so that the forest, which is appropriated to maintain the fire at the forges of Mondesir, will be soon transformed into a vast desert. In the year 1770, the people belonging to them were obliged to go a league and a half to fetch charcoal, and every year will proportionably increase that distance, so that the mutual decrease of wood and mineral will insensibly bring on the decay of this branch of commerce.

Coffee is a valuable production, and was planted in the Mauritius at six feet distance; it may be calculated that one foot will give four pounds, although a tree is not expected to produce more than a pound of coffee; for every thousand feet, a labourer is necessary for its cultivation, but however encouraging the cultivation of this may be, it will be shown hereafter, that it is now entirely neglected by the planters, for the cultivation of the sugar cane.

CHAPTER XIV.

Description of a Tour round the Island.

THE whole coast is very steep, from the Little River to the plains of St. Pierre; the soil is stony. The river Dragon, which succeeds, is fordable, as well as that of Gallet, which comes next. The coast now ceases to be steep, and it is commodious walking along the sea-side, in a large plain which leads to Tamerin Cove, and is about a quarter of a league broad.

There are various places which are no longer covered with the sea; large shells and fossils prove that it has receded from this coast. Where the sea displays itself beyond the reefs, in the offing, there is a hollow bottom or natural covered way. From the Tamerin Cove, to the Black River, (Riviere Noir) the sea-beach is steep, and along the foot of the rooks there are abundance of crabs.

After having passed the Black River, there

is a brook that falls into the sea, facing a small island called Tamarin islet; at low water it may be gained on foot, as well as the Islet Morne. Here are blocks of ferruginous rock, abounding in mineral; there is also a ridge of rocks which stretch out from the Black River, as far as Morne Brabant, which is the most windward point of the island; there is a passage behind the islet of Tamarin, and three leagues farther is Belle Ombre.

At the Point du Corail the sea enters the island between two chains of rocks formed into a peak; in stormy weather this passage is impracticable, the sea is here engulphed, and breaks in a dreadful manner.

Before you pass the Cape, there is a large bank of coral, that rises to the height of fifteen feet, and forms a kind of reef, which the sea has abandoned; from the Morne Brabant, there is an enclosure of breakers, which admit of no passage, but opposite the rivers; between the reefs and the coast, the water is very clear, and admits of seeing a forest of madreporæ, of five or six feet high; they resemble trees. Different kinds of fish, of every colour, swim amongst the branches, and others are seen that inhabit the most beautiful shells. Jacotet is a place where the sea, having penetrated inland, forms a round bay, in the middle of which is a triangular islet.

This cove is surrounded with a hill, which gives it the form of a bason, and it has no other opening but that towards the sea; at its extremity several rivulets pass over a fine sand into it, which comes from a lake of fresh water, which abounds with fish; round the lake are several small hills, which rise behind each other, in the form of an amphitheatre, and crowned with tufts of trees, in pyramidical and other pleasing shapes; behind, and above them all, the palm trees raise their tufted heads. All this mass of verdure, which rises in the midst of the mossy ground, unites with a forest, and a branch of the mountain, which stretches on the Black River. The river du Poste runs with great noise over the rocks, its waters are very transparent in dry weather, and it is fordable about a cannon shot from the mouth of it. All the coast, from the arm of the sea, near the Savannah, is rugged and unapproachable; the rivers which fall into it are very much enclosed, so that it would be impossible to proceed on horseback. After an hour's walk, this fine mossy verdure, which begins at the Morne Brabant, is seen no more, and is succeeded by a very rocky country, like the rest of the island; its grass, however, is a fine dog grass, proper for pasturage. The arm of the sea of Chalan is fordable, on a bank of sand, and penetrates inland, by so narrow a passage, that it might be enclosed, and made a large receptacle for fish. The rivers de la Chaux, and des Creoles, are very deeply embanked, between them and the principal port there are many plantations; the environs of this port, at about three quarters of a league from the river des Creoles, are covered with mango trees; the whole landscape is charming, as it is intersected by hills, covered with plantations. The air of the south-east part is of an agreeable freshness, the country beautiful and fertile.

The mouth of the Grande Reviere is about four leagues from hence; the shore is intersected with coves, where the mango trees flourish; it is probable that the seed of them was brought by the sea from some island more to windward. To the left there is a chain of high mountains, covered with wood, while verdant hillocks are scattered over the face of the country, but, though pleasing to the sight, is fatiguing to the traveller.

The Point du Diable is so named, because

the first navigators perceived, it is said, the needle to vary here without being able to account for it. The mouth of the Grande Riviére is not navigable, on account of a sand-bank that runs across it, and a cascade which it forms, about half a league up.

A quarter of a league beyond the Riviére Seche, is a path to the right, which leads towards the sea-shore, and to a lake of fresh water; there, the shore begins to be practicable, and there is a small arm of the sea of considerable depth; here and there the sand is scattered with stones, until you meet a long meadow covered with dog grass; all this part is dry and barren, the woods low and thin, and stretching to the distant mountain. This plain is three leagues over, and does not wear the appearance of fertility; a path to the left leads to Du Woos, where the rocks re-appear. The quarter of Flacq is in a good state of cultivation, and the plantations are numerous.

Near the Port de Fayette almost the whole of the coast is covered with broken rocks and mango trees.

The Cove des Aïgrettes, a considerable arm of the sea, is fordable; at some distance from hence is the Cove Requins; large beds of rock

N

are seen here pierced with a great number of round holes, a foot in diameter, some of which are of considerable depth.

From Fayette, to the river du Rampart, the flat country continues; this quarter is likewise well cultivated. Having passed the district and river called la Poudre d'Or, large woods succeed, the soil is good, but there is no water; beyond there is the river des Citronniers. In the district of Pamplemouses the ground appears to be exhausted.

CHAPTER XV.

Importation of the Hill Coolies.—Order of Her Majesty the Queen, in Council. Rules and Regulations to be observed at Mauritius, by Emigrants from British India.—Letter from the Colonial Secretary to the Commissioners for the Affairs of India.—Letter to the Governor of the Mauritius.

SINCE the emancipation of the blacks, by way of supplying the demand for labour, a considerable number of hill coolies has been brought from Hindostan, but the further importation of labourers has been suppressed by orders from the home government, the subject, however, is at the present period under legislative consideration, the result, it is to be hoped, will prove beneficial to all parties and interests. The objections raised against the importation of free labour into this, or any other colony, as approximating to slavery, may be obviated by wise and judicial measures, affording ample and complete protection to the labourers and their employers. God forbid that the great and glorious work of slave emancipation should be sullied by party feelings, or so warped by mistaken zeal, in the endeavour to serve one class, by the infliction of an act of injustice upon another· Labour is as much a marketable commodity as any thing else, and why the hill coolies should not be allowed to take theirs to the best market, we cannot imagine any just reason, so long as they can do so with safety, under the protection of the government. It would be fully verified that " example is better than precept," if the emancipated blacks had the good conduct of the Indian labourers constantly before them, not only on the score of labour, cleanliness, &c., but general good behaviour ; it would add to the general welfare and prosperity of the colony, for without such aid, the consequences to the island would be very disasterous.

Since the foregoing remarks, there has been issued an order of Her Majesty, the Queen, in Council, respecting the importation of East India labourers to the Mauritius, with the accompanying letter of the colonial secretary, to the commissioners for the affairs of India, together with the instructions forwarded to the governor general of India, and also the governor of Mauritius ; the proposed measures are of so much consequence, and vital importance to the future welfare of the colony, that it may not be deemed irrelevent to draw the attention of the reader, and all parties interested in the prosperity of the island, to the views and intentions of the government.

" ORDER of HER MAJESTY the QUEEN in COUNCIL, at the Court at Windsor, the 15th January, 1842, Present, The Queen's Most Excellent Majesty, His Royal Highness Prince Albert, &c. &c.

" Whereas it is probable, that the laws now in force in British India, for preventing the emigration of the inhabitants thereof to her Majesty's colonial possessions, will be shortly repealed, so far as regards emigration to the island of Mauritius, and that such last-mentioned emigration will be sanctioned by laws to be for that purpose enacted in India, subject to various provisions to be in such laws made for the protection of such emigrants, and for the prevention of abuses: And whereas it is probable that, amongst the provisions so to be made as last aforesaid, will be a provision for enabling the Governor General of India, to appoint at ports or places in India, officers charged with the care, protection, and superintendence of all persons proposing to emigrate as labourers from India to Mauritius: And whereas it is probable, that provision will be made by law at Mauritius, for defraying from the public revenue of that island, the expense of introducing emigration thither from British India: And whereas it is necessary that effectual provision should be made by law at Mauritius, for regulating any such expenditure, and for the prevention of abuses in the introduction of emigrants from British India into that island: It is therefore ordered by the Queen's Most Excellent Majesty, by and with the advice of her Majesty's Privy Council, that, in the event of any law being made in British India, authorizing the emigration to Mauritius of the natives of India, and repealing the restrictions now in force there in regard to such emigration, and in the event of any such laws containing provisions enabling the Governor General of India to appoint at the several ports of embarkation in India, officers charged with the protection of persons emigrating from such ports to Mauritius, the various rules and regulations comprised and set forth in the schedule to this present order subjoined, shall, within the island of Mauritius, have the force and effect of law, and shall be observed and carried into effect by all her Majesty's officers, civil and military, in Mauritius, and by all her Majesty's subjects within the same island, as to them may respectively appertain.

"And the Right Honourable Lord Stanley, one of her Majesty's principal Secretaries of State, is to give the necessary instructions herein accordingly.

(Signed) C. GREVILLE.

"The SCHEDULE referred to in the preceding Order, comprising the Rules and Regulations to be observed at Mauritius, in regard to Emigrants from British India, resorting to, and arriving at, that Island.

"1st. The Governor of Mauritius may, from time to time, nominate such persons as he shall see fit, to act as emigration agents at any port or place in India, which the Governor General of India may designate as a port or place for the embarkation of emigrants to Mauritius; and may also, from time to time, nominate a proper person to act as protector of emigrants at Mauritius.

"2nd. The remuneration to be given to any such agent in India shall not depend upon, or be regulated by, the number of the emigrants sent to Mauritius by him, but shall be in the nature of an annual salary.

"3rd. Every such emigration agent shall ascertain, by personal communication with every emigrant, previously to his or her embarkation from the port or place for which such agent shall be appointed, that such emigrant has not been induced to emigrate, by any fraud, false, nor unreasonable expectation, and is aware of the distance of Mauritius from the place where he or she is about to emigrate; and such agent shall explain the real advantages likely to be derived by such emigrants from a removal to Mauritius, and at the same time cautioning such emigrant against unreasonable and unwarrantable expectations; and such agent shall also ascertain that every such emigrant is is good health, and not incapacitated from labour by old age, bodily infirmity, or disease.

"4th. It shall not be lawful to ship on board of any ship or vessel carrying emigrants from India to Mauritius, any number of passengers exceeding the proportion of one person for every two tons of the registered burthen of such ship or vessel; and no such ship or vessel carrying emigrants, and having more than one deck, shall have less than the height of six feet, at the least, between decks; and in case such ship or vessel shall have only one deck, a platform shall be laid beneath such deck, and in such manner as to afford a space of the height of six feet at the least, and that such platform shall not be so laid as that the lower beams shall project above the same; and that no such ship or vessel shall have more than two tiers of berths; and that no such ship or vessel shall carry passengers on any such voyage to Mauritius unless there shall be an interval of six inches, at least, between the deck or platform and the floor of the lower tier, throughout the whole extent thereof; and whatever may be the tonnage of the ship or vessel, no greater number of passengers shall be taken on board of such ship or vessel, than shall be after the rate of one such person for every twelve superficial feet of the lower deck or platform, unoccupied by goods or stores, not being the personal luggage of such persons.

"5th. In the computation of the number of passengers within the meaning of these regulations, two children under the age of ten years shall be considered as equal to, and shall be reckoned as, one person only.

"6th. There shall be actually laden, and on

O

board of every ship or vessel bringing emigrants into Mauritius, at the time of departure of such ship or vessel from the port or place at which such labourers shall be embarked, good and wholesome provisions for the use and consumption of the said passengers, over and above the victualling of the crew, to the amount or in the proportions following, that is to say:—a supply of water to the amount of five gallons to every week of the computed voyage for every passenger on board such ship or vessel, such water being carried in tanks or sweet casks; and a supply of rice, bread, biscuit, flour, oatmeal, or breadstuffs, to the amount of seven pounds weight to every week of the computed voyage, for every such passenger. Provided always, that when any such ship or vessel shall be destined to call at a port or place in the course of her voyage, for the purpose of filling up her water-casks, a supply of water, at the rate before mentioned, for every week of an average voyage to such port or place of calling, shall be deemed to be a compliance with this regulation; and provided that the preceding regulation regarding food shall be deemed to have been complied with, in any case where it shall be made to appear that, by the special authority of the

Governor General of India, any other articles of food were substituted for the articles above enumerated, as being in his judgment equivalent thereto.

"7th. The number of weeks which shall be deemed necessary for the voyage to Mauritius, from any port or ports in India, shall be such as shall, from time to time, be determined by any law or ordinance to be promulgated for that purpose by the Governor General of India in Council; and according to any such law or ordinance shall and may be further determined, whether, at different periods of the year, different estimations are to be made of the probable length of any such voyage; and if, by any such law or ordinance, the removal of emigrants should, during any particular period of the year, be prohibited altogether, then any such removal during such prohibited period shall, in Mauritius, be regarded, dealt with, and punished, as an infringement of these present regulations.

"8th. Before any such ship or vessel shall be cleared out on any such voyage, the agent appointed under this ordinance for the port or place from which such ship or vessel shall be cleared out, shall survey, or cause to be surveyed by some competent person, the provisions and water herein-before required to be on board for the consumption of passengers, and shall ascertain that the same are in good and sweet condition, and also that, over and above the same, there is on board an ample supply of water and stores for the victualling of the crew of the ship or vessel; and shall also ascertain that such ship or vessel is generally reputed seaworthy, and that the directions herein-before contained for insuring the health and safety of the passengers have been complied with, and shall grant a certificate thereof, under his hand, to the master of such ship or vessel.

"9th. The master of every ship or vessel bringing emigrants to Mauritius, shall be bound to provide for and furnish to every such emigrant, and his wife and children, a sufficient quantity of good and wholesome provisions for his, her, and their daily maintenance during such voyage, and during the space of forty-eight hours next after the arrival of such ship or vessel in Mauritius.

"10th. Two copies of these regulations, authenticated by the signature of the agent at the port or place from which such emigrants shall come, shall be delivered to the master by such agent, on demand, at the time of clearance, and shall be kept on board of every ship or vessel carrying such emigrants as aforesaid; and one of such copies shall, upon request made at seasonable times to the master of the ship or vessel, be produced to any passenger for his perusal.

"11th. The master of every ship or vessel carrying emigrants from India to Mauritius shall, before clearing out such ship or vessel, deliver to such agent at the port or place from which such vessel shall be cleared out, a list in writing, together with a duplicate of the same, specifying as accurately as may be, the names, ages, and occupations of all and every the emigrants on board such ship or vessel; and such agent shall thereupon deliver to the said master the counterpart of such list, signed by such agent. And the said master shall, on the arrival of such ship or vessel at Mauritius, and previous to the disembarkation of any such emigrants, give notice of the arrival of such ship or vessel, and deliver the said counterpart of such list to the protector of emigrants herein-before mentioned; and such protector of emigrants shall forthwith proceed on board of such ship or vessel, and shall ascertain, as far as possible, by personal inspection of the ship or vessel and passengers, whether the directions herein-before contained, with regard to the situation of the berths of such ship or vessel, the proportion of the passengers to the burthens and measurements of such ship or vessel, and the maintenance of the emigrants during such passage, have been complied with. And such protector of emigrants shall personally muster such emigrants, and compare the number and names of such emigrants with the said counterparts of such list, and shall certify in writing under his hand upon such counterpart, the total number of emigrants then living and being on board of such vessel; and in case any such emigrant shall have died during the passage, or the number of names of the emigrants shall differ from the number of names stated in such counterpart, the protector of emigrants shall note such death or difference upon such counterpart, and thereupon shall grant a license under his hand for the disembarkation and landing of such emigrants

"12th. If the protector of emigrants, on such personal inspection of the ship or vessel and emigrants, shall be satisfied that the preceding regulations have been complied with, he shall grant a certificate under his hand of the arrival in Mauritius of such emigrants respectively, and the place from which, and the ship or vessel in which such emigrants shall have arrived.

"13th. No money shall be payable by the Colonial Treasurer of Mauritius in respect of any such emigrants as aforesaid, except on the warrant of the Governor of that island; which warrant shall not be issued, except on such certificate, as aforesaid, of the said protector of emigrants.

"14th. The protector of emigrants shall keep a register of all persons in respect of whom any such certificate, as aforesaid, shall be granted, and of the ship or vessel in which, the port from which, and the time at which, such person shall have arrived in this colony; a copy of which registry shall be laid before the Council of Government on the 31st day of March, the 30th of June, the 30th of September, and the 31st of December in each year.

"15th. If any ship or vessel bringing emigrants from India to Mauritius shall carry any number of passengers exceeding the proportion authorized and allowed by these regulations, a penalty of five pounds per head shall be payable in respect of each passenger so carried in excess of such proportion; or if such ship or vessel shall not be of the height between decks herein-before required; or if such a platform as herein-before directed shall not be laid and continued throughout the whole duration of any such voyage, in such manner as is herein-before required; or if there shall be more than two tiers of berths; or if there shall not be, throughout the whole duration of any such voyage, such an interval as is herein-before prescribed between the deck and the floor of the lower tier of berths; or if any such ship or vessel shall clear out and put to sea, not having on board such water and provisions as aforesaid for the use and consumption of the passengers, of the kind, and to the amount, and in the proportion herein-before directed; or if any such ship or vessel shall be cleared out before such lists of emigrants shall have been delivered, in manner and form aforesaid; or if any such lists shall be wilfully false; or if the copy of these regulations be not produced as herein-before required; or if any emigrant shall not be maintained during such voyage, and for forty-eight hours after his arrival; the master of any such ship or vessel shall, for and in respect of each and every such offence, be liable, on summary conviction before any stipendiary magistrate, at any time within the space of twelve calendar months next after the arrival of such master within the colony of Mauritius, to the payment of a fine not less than £5, nor more than £20 British sterling; and in default of payment of the fine above-mentioned, either immediately, or at the time fixed by such stipendiary magistrate at the time of making such conviction, to imprisonment for any time not less than one nor more than three calendar months.

"16th. Provided nevertheless, that nothing herein contained shall take away or abridge any right of suit or action which may accrue to any emigrant in any such ship or vessel, or to any other person, in respect of the breach or non-performance of any contract made or entered into between, or on the behalf of, any such emigrant or other person and the master, owner, or owners, of any such ship or vessel.

"17th. Provided always, that nothing in these regulations contained shall apply to any ship or vessel in the service of the Lords Commissioners of the Admiralty, or to any of her Majesty's ships of war.

"18th. No emigrant arriving from India at Mauritius shall be capable of entering into any contract of service to be performed in that

P

island, until he shall have been at least forty-eight hours on shore there, and every such contract of service made before that time shall be null and void to all intents and purposes.

"19th. No emigrant arriving from India at Mauritius, and engaging to labour in that island, shall, within Mauritius, be liable to any action, suit, or demand, for or in respect of any debt contracted, or any contract made by such emigrant, before his arrival in the said island.

"20th. No emigrant arriving from India at Mauritius shall, in Mauritius, be capable of entering into any contract for service, except for the period, in the manner, and under the superintendence which by a law in force there is required, in the case of contracts for service made by other labourers in agriculture and manufactures within the said island.

"21st. No payment shall be made from the Treasury of the said island in respect of any emigrants introduced there from India, unless on proof to the satisfaction of the Governor of Mauritius, that all rules and regulations which may be established by law in India for the advantage and protection of such emigrants have been duly complied with, such rules and regulations not being repugnant to any thing in these regulations contained.

"22nd. In every case in which the penalties hereby denounced against offences are imposed by the use of the words in the masculine gender or in the singular person, such words shall be understood as extending to the feminine gender also, and to any number of persons, unless when the opposite construction is required, in order to meet the object and to accomplish the ends, with a view to which these regulations are established and made.

(Signed) C. Greville."

"Letter from Her Majesty's Secretary of State for the Colonies.

"Sir: Downing-street, 22nd January, 1842.

"Her Majesty's Government have carefully weighed the question of permitting the introduction into Mauritius of labourers from India, and have adverted to the various despatches on that subject from yourself, which are enumerated in the margin.* Their conclusion is, that whether regard be had to the interests of the colony, or to the welfare of the labourers

* 29th December, 1840, and 24th February and 18th. May 1841.

themselves, it is desirable to revoke the existing prohibitory law. Some explanation, however, appears necessary, to prevent any misconception of the motives which have induced the confidential advisers of the Crown to adopt this conclusion.

"The abolition of slavery has rendered the British colonies the scene of an experiment, whether the staple products of tropical countries can be raised as effectually and as advantageously by the labour of freemen as by that of slaves. To bring that momentous question to a fair trial, it is requisite that no unnecessary discouragement should be given to the introduction of free labourers into our colonies. So far as it may be inevitable to obstruct such emigration, by taking effective securities that the emigrants shall be, in the fullest sense of the term, free agents, that obstruction may be justified, and no further. Without the aid to be drawn from a foreign supply of labour, much of the fixed capital at present existing in the sugar colonies, and especially in the Mauritius, will become comparatively useless. In addition to the very serious loss attendant on such an extinction of property, would be the still greater evil, that the colony must retrograde in wealth and civilization, beyond the power of recovery within any assignable period.

"To these considerations are to be added such as directly affect those for whose protection the existing restraints were imposed. In the vast population of India, poverty and distress but too often appear in the most appalling forms. Among the few resources open to the sufferers for escaping these calamities, one is emigration to Mauritius, where a constant and large demand for their labour exists. The motives for interdicting to them this relief ought to be at once clear and decisive.

"Amongst those motives, justice to the newly emancipated class has been alleged. It is maintained, that we have no moral right to introduce rivals into the market for their labour, especially when such rivals are brought there at the expense of the public revenue, a fund to which, it is said, the enfranchised negroes contribute so largely, though they have neither voice nor influence in the expenditure of it. I cannot subscribe to the justice of this reason.

"When the slaves in our colonies were emancipated, they became subject to all the duties and to all the liabilities of the free members of a free state. Industry in their callings was one of those duties, and the penalties consequent on indolence and self-indulgence were among those liabilities. I, of course, do not mean that any inoffensive member of society, who earns what is necessary for the subsistence of himself and his family, should be exposed to any punishment, in the strict and proper sense of that term, because, contenting himself with the bare necessaries of life, he consumes in idleness, time which well employed, would improve his comforts, and elevate him in the scale of society. But if a large portion of the people in any colony, contenting themselves to live in this manner, withdraw from those labours by which the community at large would be enriched and improved, they can have no reasonable ground of complaint if measures be taken by the Legislature to introduce other workmen, who will undertake the duties which they decline. In fact, by thus stimulating the indolent to a vigorous competition, the most essential benefit will, in reality, be rendered to them, in proportion as a life of successful exertion is more conducive to the welfare of man than a state of self-indulgent repose. Now, however different may be the condition of the emancipated class in many of the West India colonies, I have unfortunately your own testimony to the fact, that in Mauritius they are addicted to idle, vagrant, and unprofitable habits. No testimony can be of greater weight, because no one has exhibited a more consistent zeal for the well-being of the negro race, or vindicated their general character with more persevering earnestness.

"It is further objected to the proposed emigration of Indian labourers, that they will bring with them the Pagan superstitions of their own country, and the vices inseparable from them; that the scheme tends to establish an inferior and degraded caste, with all its attendant evils, social and moral, and that thus, manual labour, by being associated with ideas of contempt and aversion, will lose the honourable estimation which ought to attach to it.

"Whatever may be the force of these considerations, in reference to colonies inhabited exclusively by men of European origin, or by men possessing the blessings of Christianity, knowledge, and civilization, they are scarcely applicable to the case of Mauritius. I fear it is not true, in fact, that the character of the labouring population in that island is such as to be impaired by the proposed association with the natives of India. Many thousands of those people are already settled there, and living in the immediate vicinity of large bodies of the African race, not more advanced than themselves in religious knowledge and in the arts of civilized life.

"Finally, it has been urged as a reason against permitting the removal of Indian labourers to our colonies, that the distance is, in general, such as to render altogether illusory the promise or the prospect of their ultimate return to their native land. Such is the comparative vicinity of the continent of India, and so constant the commercial intercourse with Mauritius, that an Indian labourer might in that island be at a much easier distance from home than he would be in many parts of the continent of India itself; and, in point of fact, many of those who have already fulfilled their contracts in Mauritius have returned to India, and having visited their families, and deposited with them the amount of their accumulations, would gladly enter into fresh engagements, were they not debarred by the existing law.

"But, in discussing this question, we must not forget the impotency of restrictive laws, to arrest effectually any trade in which the interests of a whole community are involved, and to which no sense of moral obligation is opposed. Such is precisely the case with regard to the introduction of labourers into Mauritius. It is evident from your reports, that the urgency of the demand is triumphing over the mere legal obstacles which interdict the practice, and that an increase of the labouring population is in progress, by recruits from the adjacent countries, and even from India itself, through foreign settlements. The choice must therefore be made between some stringent law closing the ports of the island to all persons seeking employment there, and the admission of such persons, upon some system carefully devised for the prevention to the utmost possible extent of such abuses as may reasonably be apprehended. In this alternative her Majesty's Government prefer the latter course.

"With a view, therefore, to regulate the introduction of Indian labourers into Mauritius, her majesty in Council has been pleased to make the Order of which I enclose a copy. It has not been thought right to leave this subject to the colonial Legislature, partly because it is one on which her Majesty's Government have the advantage of a wider observation and a more extensive experience than could be commanded within the colony itself, and partly because the effects of the law will extend beyond the limits of Mauritius, although the direct operation of it will, of course, be confined to that island.

"The Order presupposes (and, of course, not without sufficient reason) the enactment by the Legislature of India of a law repealing the existing prohibitory laws in force there, taking due security for the protection of the emigrants before their departure; granting to the Governor General the power of sanctioning, upon application from the colony, certain ports of embarkation, and providing for the establishment at every port of an official protector of the emigrants.

"The Order further presupposes the grant by the Mauritius Legislature of funds, to be paid as bounties on the importation of emigrants. I infer from your despatches, that there will be no disinclination to make such grants, but the reverse; but it will be necessary, also, that provision should be made by the colonial law for remunerating such official protectors as may be appointed by the Indian Government. At each port of embarkation an emigration agent must also be stationed on behalf of the Government of Mauritius; and within the island itself must be established an officer, to be entitled the 'Protector of Emigrants.' For the remuneration of these officers also provision must be made from the colonial treasury. The annual salary of the Protector of Emigrants should not be less than £800.

"The duties of the officers to be employed by your Government are, I trust, clearly defined in the Order in Council. They will, in general, be to prevent any fraud or misrepresentation in inducing labourers to emigrate; to ascertain that the emigrants are persons fit for the service and properly selected; to take security for the sea-worthiness of the ships employed; for their being properly victualled, and against their being over-crowded. For the breach of these regulations pecuniary penalties are provided; but the more effective penalty will be the entire loss of bounty, in the event of the infringement of them. The Order further forbids any contracts for service being made until forty-eight hours after the emigrant shall have actually landed; limits the duration of such contracts; determines the manner of making, enforcing, and cancelling them; and exempts any emigrant from liability to serve, in respect of any debt which he may have contracted before reaching the island.

"Such are the main objects of this Order. You will promulgate it as soon as it shall reach you; but until you shall have received intelligence from India of the repeal of the restrictive laws in force there, you will not be able to carry it into execution.

"The system of protection would, however, be defective and inadequate to its object, if it should rest merely on the provisions of this Order in Council; securities will, of course, be also taken by the Government of India, against any deceptions or ill-usage to which the emigrants might be exposed before their departure. The Governor General in Council will, of course, determine the nature of these securities according to his own discretion, and with the aid of his local knowledge. To the protector of emigrants the charge and superintendence of the whole system will probably be committed by the law to be made in India, so far, at least, as concerns the interest of the Indian labourers while yet remaining within their own country. Among the regulations thus to be established, will probably be such as may be requisite for maintaining a due proportion of sexes, and for preventing the improper separation of families, or the desertion of helpless women and children. It remains that I should notice the provision to be made for securing to emigrants arriving from India the means of return. Her Majesty's Government are of opinion, that in the case of such persons it is not enough to rely on the forethought and frugality of the emigrant himself to secure the means of return, and to retain the unfettered power of so employing them when the proper period arrives. We think that provision must be made for these objects by other and more certain means. The accompanying Order in Council is silent on the subject, because it could not have been adjusted in that instrument without the direct imposition by the Royal authority of a local tax or of a charge on the local revenue, which we are, of course, anxious if possible to avoid. But the same object may be effected by other and less inconvenient methods. You will not propose to the local legislature the grant of any sum by way of bounty on the introduction of emigrants from India, nor assent to any such grant, if proposed by any member of that body, unless the grant be connected with the appropriation of such a sum as may be presumably necessary for defraying the expenses of the return of the emigrant after the lapse of five years from his arrival. Thus there will be in your hands the means of defraying the charge of the return to India of every Indian emigrant who may have been introduced at the public expense. But even this will not be sufficient. Before you assent to any grant of public money for this service, you must take care that the grant is connected with due legal provision; that at the end of five years from the arrival of each emigrant he should be free to quit the colony, notwithstanding any unfulfilled engagements by which he may then be bound for the discharge of any service; so that all hirings must at the arrival of that period cease, whatever may be their duration, if, with a view to his return home, it shall be the pleasure of the emigrant then to bring them to a close.

"I have entered thus fully into the whole of this subject, because it was of no light importance, and because the measure we adopted may perhaps be quoted as a precedent for similar measures elsewhere, which would be beyond the reach of the principles on which her Majesty's Government have acted in this case. To prevent as far as possible any such misapprehension, I have thought it right to enter into a statement of those principles, and of the practical consequences deduced from them.

I have, &c.

(Signed) STANLEY.

" Sir Lionel Smith, Bart.,
&c. &c. &c."

" LETTER from the SECRETARY to the BOARD OF COMMISSIONERS for the AFFAIRS of INDIA.

" SIR : India Board, February, 1842.

" I am directed by the Commissioners for the Affairs of India to transmit to you a copy of a letter dated the 27th ultimo, with its enclosures, which the Board have received from her Majesty's Secretary of State for the Colonies, on the subject of permitting the emigration of labourers from the East-Indies to the Island of Mauritius.

" The Board request that you will move the Court of Directors to cause the draft of a despatch, with reference to these papers, to be prepared and submitted to the Board with the least possible delay.

I have the honour to be, &c.

(Signed) J. EMERSON TENNENT.

J. C. Melville, Esq."

" LETTER to the GOVERNMENT of INDIA,
Dated the 22nd March, 1842.
(Legislative Department—No. 4, of 1842.)

" 1. In our despatch of the 29th September last (No. 22) we informed you, that we had received the minutes recorded by the Governor General and by the several Members of Council, relative to the Report of the Committee on Hill Coolies, with the subsequent information obtained on the same subject.

" 2. We went on in that despatch to observe as follows :—

" 'From these documents we infer that, 'though differing widely as to the extent to 'which alteratious should be made in the pro-'visions of Act XIV. of 1839, prohibiting the 'emigration of labourers from India to any 'British or foreign colony, you are all of 'opinion that that Act should be subject to 'revision and be more or less modified. You 'are aware, however, that the subject has 'engaged the particular attention of Parlia-'ment, without whose sanction we cannot 'authorize you to withdraw the absolute pro-'hibition imposed by that Act.

" 'The grounds suggested in the papers 'now before us, on which it may eventually 'be deemed expedient to permit the emigra-'tion of labourers not under any contract, or 'the emigration of artizans, or emigration at 'the discretion, and under the express sanction 'of Government, will, we doubt not, receive 'full consideration, together with the rules 'proper to be applied thereto, and the advan-'tages which might be anticipated mutually 'to the colonists and to the labourers them-'selves; for the present, however, the Act 'must remain in force."

"3. In pursuance of the views above stated, the Report of the Committee on Hill Coolies, and your several minutes thereupon, were communicated to Parliament; but we have been apprized by the Commissioners for the Affairs of India that, under the information on the subject which has now been furnished by your Government and by that of Mauritius, her Majesty's Ministers do not deem it necessary to apply for any legislative enactment in this country, with a view to such modification of Act XIV. of 1839 as may be found adviseable.

"4. We transmit to you the accompanying copy of a letter* from the Secretary to the Board of Commissioners for the Affairs of

* Dated 5th February 1842.

R

India, and copies of the several documents therewith received, on the subject of modifying the provisions of that Act as far as relates to the colony of Mauritius. You will perceive the anxiety manifested by her Majesty's Government that the act of emigration, in each individual instance, shall be one of perfect free-will; that the health, comfort, and welfare of the emigrant shall be fully provided for, both on the passage and in the colony; and that the emigrant shall have the means of returning to India whenever he may be desirous of doing so. You will also discover from the accompanying documents, that the arrangements to be adopted for the purpose of securing these objects are mainly left to your judgment and discretion, and that it is perfectly open to you altogether to prevent the contemplated change of the law, if you should consider it hostile to the real welfare of the people of India.

"5. The primary consideration with us, as well as with you, in this matter is that a project intended to promote the advantage of certain classes of the people of India, by allowing them free command of their labour, shall not be perverted to their injury; and we feel perfect confidence in committing to you the duty of establishing proper safeguards for that purpose. You are prepared for the discharge of this duty by the laborious examination which this subject has received at your hands, and by your ready access to whatever more full or more recent information may be of use in guiding your judgment. Lord Auckland adverts in his minute to the early expiration of the contracts of several thousands of Indian labourers at Mauritius, and to the probable return of many of them to their own country, which would place ample means of information of that nature within your reach.

"6. In determining upon the measures to be adopted, you will, of course, have regard to the manner in which they may affect the emigration of labourers from the foreign settlements in India as well as from our own territories.

"7. With reference to the accompanying papers, you will lose no time in apprizing the Governor of the Mauritius of the result of your deliberations.

"8. We have only further to desire that, in the event of your deeming it proper, under the authority now conveyed to you, to pass any law permitting the emigration of labourers from India to the Mauritius, you will carefully watch its operation, and will repeal or modify it without delay, if its provisions shall not prove effectual in affording, in all respects, the intended security for the comfort and welfare of the emigrants.

We are, &c.

(Signed) G. LYALL,
J. L. LUSHINGTON,
London, &c. &c. &c."
22nd March, 1842.

"LETTER from the SECRETARY to the EAST INDIA COMPANY.

"SIR: East-India House, 23rd February, 1842.

"1. I have laid before the Court of Directors of the East-India Company, your letter of the 5th instant, transmitting a copy of a letter dated the 27th ultimo, with its enclosures, which the Board of Commissioners have received from her Majesty's Secretary of State for the Colonies, on the subject of permitting the emigration of labourers from the East-Indies to the Island of Mauritius; with reference to which papers you convey the request of the Board, that the Court will cause the draft of a despatch to be prepared and submitted with the least possible delay.

"2. In reply, I am commanded to request that you will remind the Board, that, in a despatch to the Government of India dated the 29th September last, the Court stated that this subject had engaged the particular attention of Parliament, without whose sanction the Court could not authorize the withdrawal of the absolute prohibition imposed by Act No. XIV. 1839.

"3. In reference to this communication, and observing by the votes of the House of Commons of the 4th instant, that leave has been given to bring in a 'Colonial Passengers' Bill,' the Court would suggest the expediency (should it be the intention of Government to take the opinion of Parliament upon the subject) of postponing any instructions to the Government of India until that course shall have been adopted.

I have, &c.

(Signed) J. C. Melvill,
Secretary.

J. E. Tennent, Esq., M.P.,
&c. &c. &c.

CHAPTER XVI.

Division of the Island of Mauritius.

No. 1.—Municipality of the North-west Port; extends from the River des Lataniers, the boundary of the municipality of Moka, to the Grande Rivere.

No. 2.—Municipality of Pamplemousses; from the River des Lataniers, the limits of the municipality of Moka, of the three Islets, and of the Riviere du Rampart, as far as the great bay.

No. 3.—Municipality du Rampart; from the Grande Baie, the boundary of the municipality des Pamplemousses, and of the Three Islets, as far as the French River.

No. 4.—Municipality of Flacq; from the French River, the boundary of the municipality of the three islets to the Riviere Seche.

No. 5.—Municipality of the Three Islets; from la Riviere Seche, the boundary of the municipality of Flacq, of the Rampart, of

Pamplemousses, and of Moka, to the Deep River, or Great River of the Great Port.

No. 6.—Municipality of the Great Port Bourbon, or Port of Fraternity; from Great River, the boundary of the municipality of the Three Islets, of Moka, and of the Plaines Wilhems, to the River du Poste.

No. 7.—Municipality of the Savannah; from the River du Poste, the boundary of the Plaines Wilhems, to the Bay of the Cape.

No. 8.—Municipality of the Plains of St. Pierre and Black River; from the Bay of the Cape, the boundary of the Savannah, and of the Plaines Wilhems, to the Little River.

No. 9. Municipality of Plaines Wilhems; from the Little River, the boundary of the municipality of the Black River, of the Savannah, of the Great Port, and of Moka, to the Great River of Port North-west.

No. 10.—The municipality of Moka; comprised between those of the North-west Port, of the Plaines Wilhems, of the Great Port, of the Three Islets, and of Pamplemousses.

CHAPTER XVII.

Observations on the Isle of France by M. de Cossigny.—Remarks of the Abbe Raynal.

" The Isle of France, from its two ports, the one to windward, and the other to leeward of the island, though they have hitherto been too much neglected, will become the mother of the colonies which France ought to establish in the East Indies, if she is anxious to increase her commerce and power. This colony, which was originally settled in 1722, is not yet arrived to that degree of strength to which there is every reason to presume that it will one day attain; its soil, which is in general fertile and ferruginous, seems to have been formed from the ruins of a volcano, at a very remote period. Lava is to be met with almost every-where, and I have on my estate a bed of volcanic ashes.* The whole land is covered

* M. de Cossigny was Governor of the Isle of France in the year 1791; he was a man full of knowledge and philanthrophy.

with fine trees, among which there were many fit for building, in a profusion that proves the fertility of the soil; two successive harvests in the course of the year, confirm its claim to that character. The most useful vegetables of the four quarters of the world have been collected in the national garden, which for these seven-and-twenty years have been under the direction of M. Cére. In doing justice to the zeal, intelligence, and activity of this excellent person, I do no more than repeat the merited eulogiums which the public voice has lavished upon him.

"The Isle of France was formerly exposed to the ravages of locusts, few of these noxious insects, however, have been seen here since the year 1770. It is stated that the martins, a bird brought here from India, and which have multiplied in a very extraordinary manner, have destroyed them. It is certain that these birds feed upon them with avidity, when they are just produced, and before they have wings. This colony, considered as an anchoring place, is well situated for the commerce of the East Indies; it furnishes the ships with all kinds of refreshments and provisions, and the means of recovering their crews; the air is healthy, and the water excellent; considered

S

as a port, it furnishes a shelter for the ships, with every necessary accommodation to careen, refit, and equip them. It might in this respect become an entrépot for the commerce of the East Indies. This was the project of M. de la Bourdonnais. Considered in an agricultural view, it would furnish commerce with valuable objects of exportation, such as sugar, coffee, cotton, indigo, fine spice, &c.: as a military station, it can contain in its bosom a large number of land and sea forces.

"I do declare it to be my opinion that the Isle of France will one day astonish Europe and Asia by its riches, the variety and abundance of its productions, and the resources of its numerous population: in the course of time it will have very great influence on the commerce of Europe in the Indies, and incalculably extend the advantages of the nation who possesses it, in that quarter of the globe.

"A colony whose soil is fertile, the air healthy, and whose position is so fortunate, both for the operations of commerce, and the plans of policy, must necessarily arise from its present state of mediocrity. It has not as yet acquired all that a sagacious minister, a wise administration, a constant and well directed labour of the colonists, and time, the operations of which perfects everything, may procure it. Nature had clothed its soil with extensive forests, but industry and patriotism have collected here the greatest part of the useful productions of hot countries, as well as many of the natives of temperate climates, which flourish with luxuriance, so that at present it has more useful plants collected, than any other part of the known world. M. de la Bourdonnais, that great man whom history already mentions with the eulogiums which he so well deserves, that great general, mariner, administrator, merchant, and agriculturist, considered the Isle of France as the key of the Indian commerce of his nation, as the bulwark of its settlements in Asia, and as the means of future conquests; he did more, —he proved the exactness of his last views by keeping the English fleet from the coast of Coromandel, and by besieging and taking Madras.

His object was to make the Isle of France the entrepot of the Indian commerce of France, and as a place of arms for its land and sea forces. His idea was to make it an agricultural, commercial, and military settlement. Let us add another respectable authority:— Were it not for the Isle of France, says the author of the Philosophical History, the French settlements in India could not be protected. He also adds, that the Isle of France will always be ready to give assistance to Pondicherry, or to act offensively, according as circumstances may require; indeed everything may be expected from the Isle of France, when it shall have gained that degree of prosperity to which it must one day arrive, when its cultivation shall be more extended, and its population more numerous, although it has been, as it were, abandoned to itself since the Revolution; the English have not thought proper to direct their attacks against it, they preferred the conquests of the Dutch settlements; they are, however, deeply interested in rendering themselves masters of it, in order to secure the power in Indostan, their new conquests, and their commerce, which this island interrupted by its privateers. Policy, says the Abbe Raynal, forsees, that if the Isle of France were abandoned, the English would drive all foreign nations out of the seas of Asia, and would possess themselves of all the riches of these vast countries.

CHAPTER XVIII.

Hurricanes.—Indications.—Description of an Hurricane in the Mauritius by M. Rochon.

Hurricanes are so called, from the Indian word hurica, which signifies the devil; immediately previous to the commencement of an hurricane, the wind and sea become suddenly calm, the summits of the mountains covered with thick clouds, the air darkened, the atmosphere oppressive, and the sky gloomy; soon the sky seems on fire with horrible lightnings, accompanied with dreadful thunder, the birds and animals in a state of disturbance; sometimes the winds blow a little from the south-east, with a heavy rolling of the sea from the west; suddenly the winds commence with impetuous force, rooting up the strongest trees, and destroying every thing within their vortex; the winds then traverse the whole round of the heavens, and blow from every point of the compass.

M. Rochon, in his account of an hurricane, states that " it is absolutely necessary to have been an eye-witness of an hurricane, to form a just idea of such a formidable phenomenon. It is almost always accompanied with rain, thunder, and earthquake; the atmosphere is on fire, and the wind blows with equal violence from every part of the horrizon. An hurricane is a kind of water spout, which seems to threaten the spot over which it hangs with an entire subversion, while vessels are actually becalmed at a small distance from its explosion. If the swiftness of the wind exceeds one hundred and fifty feet in a second, nothing can then resist its force; the largest trees are torn up by the roots, the most solid buildings are thrown down, nor can the weight of anchors, the strength of cables, nor the strongest hold of the ground, secure safety to vessels, which are dashed to pieces on the shore, unless they are thrown on a bed of mud. I saw the maintopmast borne away from the Mars, of sixty-four guns, and shattered to pieces. An extraordinary variation of the barometer is the only sign of an approaching hurricane, in the seas between the tropics. Previous to the hurricane, in February, the sudden descent of the mercury filled me with alarm, as well as M. Poivre, who requested the port captain to come to his house; this officer, who had been an eye-witness of the hurricane in 1761, was not equally surprized with us at the variation of the barometer, and told us that there were more certain indications; twenty-four hours, he said, before the hurricane, you will see the black cloud descend from the mountain, and declare the approaching storm, besides, the setting of the sun will decide the measures I shall employ on the occasion. But neither the entreaties of M. Poivre, nor my observations, were capable of changing his opinions, and though the mercury continued to descend, as the sun set in great beauty and serenity, the port captain left us perfectly satisfied and free from alarm, as to any threatening danger. He had long served on board the Company's ships, and seemed to pity us for giving so much importance to the predictions of our barometer. It is very difficult indeed to soften the obstinacy of a man, who knowing nothing but the practical part of his art, treats with disregard the instructions of theory.

"The hurricane however declared itself at seven in the evening, which was an hour after sun set; before nine, all the ships were driven on shore, except the Ambulante, store ship, and a small corvette called the Verd-Galand, but in a violent gust of wind the former was driven out to sea, and the latter was sunk.

"The Ambulante, without sails, helm, or provisions, and with a detachment of the Irish regiment de Clare, who were on board, was driven about for upwards of twelve hours, at the mercy of the winds, and, after being carried by their variation round the island, was miraculously thrown upon the only plaee where, in such a violent tempest, it would have been possible for the persons on board to save themselves. The violence of the winds, and the force of the torrents, renders it impracticable for any one to quit the shelter he has sought, or the spot where he happens to be, at the commencement of the storm. The horror of these hurricanes is greatly aggravated by the total impossibility of affording or receiving assistance It lasted about eighteen hours without interruption, and with undeviating violence; neither the heavy rain, thunder, or lightning were in the least interrupted by the violence of the wind, but at three in the afternoon the mercury, which had descended twenty-five lines, remained stationary some minutes, and then began to reascend, from thence the tornadoes ceased, the wind became more regular, and at six in the evening it was possible to give some assistance to those who were shipwrecked. From the ravages of the hurricane the established communications between the different parts of the island were altogether interrupted by the fall of trees, and the abundance of rain ; three weeks elapsed before any intelligence was reccived of the Ambulante, which had been shipwrecked about the distance of six leagues from Port Louis. All the harvests were destroyed, and the vessels were in such a state as to require the utmost exertions to repair them. These vessels were no sooner equipped than they were despatched to Madagascar, to fetch provisions and necessaries of every kind. M. Poivre had, with his superior foresight and precaution, ordered several vessels to winter at the Cape of Good Hope, which were sent off with abundance of supplies as soon as the disastrous state of the Isle of France had reached the government. This relief saved the colony, as it arrived immediately after the hurricane, whose fresh devastations had sunk the hope, and conquered the resolution of the unfortunate inhabitants. The damage sustained by the vessels in the port, by the violence of

T

the waves, and the force of the winds, in the second hurricane, were much less than in the first. The variation of the barometer announced the danger, and every one employed the means he possessed for his security and preservation.

CHAPTER XIX.

Island of Rodriguez.—First Residents.—Soil.—Trees.—The Solitaire; singular Habits of the Bird.—Ambergris; the Production of it. The present State of the Island.

The Island of Rodriguez, being particularly connected with the Mauritius, the following account, containing a relation of the first remarkable events which happened there, naturally presents itself as an appropriate link in the chain of the description of the Island of Mauritius and ies dependencies.

This island is situated in Lat. 19. 41 S., Long. 63. 20 East, is about twenty-six miles long, and twelve broad, possessing a mild climate; the country is mountainous, and in many places full of rocks and large stones, which cover the surface, though there is other parts where the soil is excellent, and calculated to produce fruit trees, and vegetables of every kind; land turtle are in great abundance, sea turtles are also plentiful. There is an abundance of fish of various kinds, those taken in deep water beyond the reefs has been found to be poisonous, while those which are taken in the more shallow parts are excellent, particularly the Pierre Bas; the red and gray mullet, and a fish that resembles a whiting, and which the French call Mort au Chein. On the northern side of this island there is a bay, which affords excellent anchorage, and a secure shelter, for ships of all dimensions. There are also ample supplies of wood; and excellent water may be obtained with the greatest facility. It is high water at the new and full moon, at three quarters past twelve at noon, N. by E. and S. by W. The spring-tide rises from four to five feet perpendicular height, and the common tides seldom more than a foot. Vessels may enter the port with safety from the end of May to the beginning of December.

The first residents on the island were a few refugee Protestants from France, whom M. du Quesne, in the year 1690, prevailed on the Dutch government to send in a frigate, in order to form an establishment in the Island of Bourbon, in favour of the Protestant refugees of France; they however did not land there, as they unexpectedly found that the French were in possession of it, they proceeded to this island, where they found more resources than they had any reason to suppose, but which were not unaccompanied with sufferings and misfortunes. One of these adventurers, M. le Guat, has left a relation respecting their proceedings; wherein he states that "the island had a very inviting appearance, both at a distance, and on our near approach to it; this little new world seemed to us a seat of delight, though we did not see so many birds as appeared on the shore of the Island of Tristan; nor was the air so perfumed with flowers as when we passed the Island of Bourbon, about a month before; but the aspect of this island was so delightful, that we could scarce satisfy ourselves with gazing at the little mountains of which it is composed, covered as they were with large and beautiful trees.

"The rivulets, whose course we could discern as they sank in the vallies, after expanding in various branches over a considerable space of country, which I shall not call either a plain or forest, though either denomination might be applied to it, flowed immediately before us into the sea. We admired the secret and extraordinary operations of Providence, which, after having permitted us to be ruined in our own country, and to be cruelly driven from it, had at last suffered us to dry up our tears in this earthly paradise, to which we had been conducted, and where it depended upon ourselves alone to be rich, free, and happy, by employing our tranquil life in the calm enjoyment of what we possessed, in glorifying the author of all good, and advancing our final salvation. We established ourselves to the N.N.W. of the island, in a fine valley, and near a large brook of excellent water, but it was not until we had examined every part that we preferred the spot of which I shall now give a description. A small river, that rises near the middle of the island, and about four or five thousand paces above the site of our huts, forms, by falling from rock to rock, a succession of cascades, basons, and pieces of water, that would adorn the gardens of a prince.

"In warm and dry seasons it receives but little water from its source; but, at all times, the tide keeps it full to the spot where the land begins to rise. This side of the river is, in general, less elevated than the other, and is sometimes inundated by the rains.

"Pierre Thomas, one of our pilots, determined to inhabit a small island formed by the brook, he accordingly built his hut, made his little garden, and threw a couple of bridges over the branches of the stream; during an inundation he used to roost in a tree, and always made his situation pleasant to himself, as well as agreeable to his companions; he sang, played upon the flute, and was the only person among us who smoked tobacco; when his stock was exhausted, he supplied it with the dried leaves of certain trees in the island. The hut nearest to this island was that of M. de la Haye, he was by profession a goldsmith, and had constructed a forge, so that he was obliged to make his house somewhat larger than the rest. The huts were from ten to fifteen feet square, according to the fancy of the builders; the trunks of the Lataniers formed the walls, and the leaves of the same tree covered the roofs; the huts were at some distance from each other, and a palisade enclosed our gardens; near the water was the town-house, where our little republic used to assemble to deliberate, principally concerning the affairs of the kitchen. This building was twice the size of the others, here our food was prepared, and under a large tree beside the hut, we used to eat it; this tree spread its thick branches over us, and defended us from the heat of the climate; it was in the trunk of this tree that we scooped a niche, as a receptacle for those memorials which I shall particularize hereafter. On the other side of the water, exactly opposite to the building which we call the public hotel, was the public garden, it was a spot of fifty or sixty feet square, surrounded by a palisade about six feet high, and formed in such a manner as to prevent the smallest tortoises from passing through it. The hut of M. le Guat was situate between two flower gardens, and rested against a large tree, which protected it on the side of the sea. This tree yielded a fruit which bore some resemblance to an olive, and whose kernel was a favorite food of the parroquets. A little lower and nearer the water was the abode of M. de la Case.* On the other side of the rivulet, between the little island and the public garden, M. Testard erected his habitation; his sad fate will be related, and the most sincere regret, which will ever accompany the remembrance of that amiable and gallant man. M. M. B**le and Boyer inhabited the same dwelling, which

* The names of La Case and Testard continue to be well known in the islands of Madagascar, Mauritius and Bourbon.

they had erected at a small distance from the brook, and nearer to the sea. The latter of them died in this island, and his ashes repose there; the epitaph which was inscribed on his distant tomb declares our opinion of his excellence; the former still lives; when we were at this island he was not more than twenty years of age, but while he possessed the vivacity natural to his period of life, he had the composure, mildness, and discretion of a more prolonged experience; he had received a good education, and the advantages he had derived from it he was ready to communicate to all around him. It was principally to his inventive genius that we were enabled to construct the vessel, which will be hereafter mentioned, as well as to succeed in the manufacture of hats, which proved so useful to us. I shall also remark, that excepting Pierre Thomas and R. Anselin, who were of low origin, we were all of us superior to want, and had not thrown ourselves through despair on a desert island, or from not having a place whereon to rest the soles of our feet: many of the party were persons of good family, and some property, but as this colony of M. du Quesne made some noise, and we were young, healthy, active, and without any incumbrances, the spirit of enterprize induced us to make the voyage. The trees which were scattered about our little town, were the remains of a much larger number, which we thought proper to clear away; this was no very difficult task, as the soil is very light, and the roots easily separated from it. When we had finished our humble habitations, the captain of the frigate, who had remained fifteen days in the road, bade adieu to us, when he had provided the necessary refreshments; he did not however think proper to leave every thing which had been designed for us; nor did we fail, in our letters to Holland, to give him the character which he deserved, but, as we were afterwards informed, he very discreetly did not deliver them to the person to whom they were addressed.

"He however left us a quantity of biscuit, with fire-arms and ammunition, tools for agriculture, saws, hatchets, and the necessary implements for building; some household utensils, mills, fishing nets, and linen; besides each individual had his own baggage and private stores. The medicine chest, by some inadvertence, as may be supposed, was not brought on shore. Pierre Thomas, who has been already mentioned, had quarelled with the captain, and being afraid of returning with him, wished to remain in the island, so that he would have repaired the loss of one of our companions, who died at sea, near Mascaregnas, but the captain, on the very eve of his departure, came on shore and took away two of our companions, Jaques Guiguies and Pierrot, so that the whole of the little colony consisted of no more than eight persons.

"The air of Rodriguez is very pure and wholesome, and as a proof of it, not one of us was sick during the two years we remained there, notwithstanding the great difference of climate and mode of nourishment.

"The island, as it has been already observed, consists of a succession of hills, of various and pleasing shapes, which are covered with flourishing trees, whose perpetual verdure, of the most pleasing scenery, and being seldom embarrassed with underwood, form delightful groves, which, while they afford a most refreshing shade, break the views, some of which embrace a large extent of ocean, into pleasing and magnificent prospects. The vallies that serpentine between the hills, possess the finest soil in the world; it may be said to be entirely composed of decayed trees and leaves, which being reduced to a kind of compost, are washed by time down the sides of the hills, to enrich the valleys beneath them; this soil, being very light, requires little or no culture, and is pregnant with fertility. The valleys are shaded with different kind of palms, the ebony, and various other trees, whose branches and foliage do not yield in beauty to those of the finest trees in Europe. In the bottom of these valleys there are streams of limpid water, which are plentifully supplied from perennial springs, in the middle of the island; and, had the course of these rivulets been expressly directed by the hand of art, to water this little country, they could not have been contrived with better effect; but to their beauty may be added the utility they afford to the spot, which they alike refresh and adorn.

" Seven waterfalls may be seen at the same time, tumbling down from the rocks, into as many basins, and uniting to form one delightful stream. These waters abound with eels of a very extraordinary size, and exquisite taste.

" The valleys, which are fertilized by these beautiful rivulets, insensibly widen as they approach the sea, till they extend sometimes into plains of two thousand yards broad, whose soil, to the depth of eight or ten feet, possess the most fertile qualities; they are also covered with those delightful groves which have already been mentioned, beneath whose shade, in the noon-tide of the hottest season, the air possesses a most agreeable and enlivening freshness. The trees shoot up their tufted tops to the same height, and, interlacing their branches with each other, form a succession of leafy canopies, which bend, as it were, into a large platform of never failing verdure, while the stems, like so many strait and lofty pillars, at once support and nourish it; an unrivalled example of the architecture of nature. At the same time, the greatest part of the trees which adorn this little paradise, are not less useful to the service than gratifying to the senses of man. The different kinds of palm tree are so many astonishing magazines to supply the necessaries of life; their fruit is excellent, while the juice which flows from their trunks is, without any preparation, a very delicious and salutary beverage. The leaves of some of them are esculent, and of a grateful taste, while others bear a resemblance to linen and silken stuffs. There are more than thirty kinds of palm trees. It may be proper, however, to give some general account of those which we found in the Isle of Rodriguez: they are in general about thirty or forty feet in height, their trunk is strait and without leaves, but covered with a kind of sharp scales, which are somewhat raised at the point; others have a smooth bark. At the upper end of the trunk grows the branches of palm leaves, which hang down like so many plumes of feathers; beneath these branches grow long clusters of fruit, which is green, and of the size, as well as the shape, of an egg; it is known by the name of date. In the centre of this large leafy plumage, and on the summit of the trunk, grows what is called the cabbage; it is not visible, as the branches rise all around, and overtop its situation. It is composed of tender leaves, which adhere closely to each other, and form a mass like that of cabbage; it is about two feet in height, and of the same thickness as the trunk; the large outward leaves of this mass are white, sweet, supple, and strong; they may be used as goat skins. when skilfully dressed; or linen, satin, napkins and towels, such is their various utility. The membranes or leaves of the heart are tender and crisp, like that of a luttuce; it may be eaten raw, and is in taste like a nut, and forms an admirable ragout, when dressed with the fat and liver of the land turtle. The nectar of the island is the palm wine, so well known throughout the Indies; there are two modes employed to obtain it; we sometimes made a hole, about five inches in diameter, in the trunk of the tree, at the height of about six feet, and a vessel being suspended under it, was soon filled with this pleasant liquor; at other times the cabbage wss scooped out of the tree, by which operation a cistern was formed on the top, from whence, two or three times a day, the juice might be drawn; either way the liquor was equally good; but, in order to spare the trees, the first method is the best, as, after the reservoir, formed by the removal of the cabbage, has furnished its liquor for a month, the tree becomes so exhausted as to decline and die; but the incision, if not made too deep, is not attended with any fatal effects; the liquor will not however flow from one aperture more than four days, when the tree must be left to recover its strength; besides, if a very large wound should be made, it may weaken the trunk to such a degree as to disable it from resisting the hurricanes.

"The Latanier (Corypha umbraculifera, Linn.) is placed by botanists in the class of palm trees. In the Island of Rodriguez this tree has a strait trunk, formed, as it appears, of a succession of large rings, of equal thickness, with a smooth bark ; at the top there is a cabbage, similar to that which has been just described, at the bottom of which several large leaves shoot forth, whose stalks are six or seven feet in length ; these leaves are strong and thick, and resemble an open fan ; some of them are eight feet in diameter, so that they form an excellent covering for houses ; they may also be shaped into hats and umbrellas. The stalk, which is hollow, is four fingers broad, and upwards of an inch thick, and rather round on the sides ; the extremity of it, which springs from the tree, and in a great measure embraces it, presents a large and concave shape, which is sometimes more than a foot in diameter, is about the thickness of a crown piece, and was made to serve the purpose of plates and dishes ; the exterior rind of this stalk may be employed for ropes, and the fibres of the interior one will serve as a sewing thread ; it appears, indeed, that it might be woven into linen, if the filaments were properly prepared.

"There is also in the Isle Rodriguez the Indian fig tree (ficus indica), its branches extend in a circular form, and are so thick as be impenetrable to the solar rays. Some of these trees are so large, that two or three hundred persons may take shelter under them; this circumstance arises from the peculiar property of the branches, which bend down to the earth, take root there, and form a progeny of stems, that by shooting forth new branches, compose this vast extent of shade; the inhabitants of the East hold this tree in great veneration: according to Boulaye le Gaut, this tree is called the Sacred Kasta, and is held in such high estimation by the devotees, because their god Kan is said to have diverted himself with playing the flute beneath the umbrage of its wide spreading branches. The same author adds, that the inhabitants do not venture to rob it of a single leaf, from the apprehension that death will inevitably follow within a year of such a violation. He also refers his readers to what Herodotus and Quintus Curtius have written concerning it; Tavernier also mentions, that it is called Lul by the Persians, but that the Franks gave it the name of Banian, because the penitent Faquiers, and Banians, perform their devotions within its bowers. M. de Rochefort calls it Parcturier, in his natural history of the Antilles. According to his description, the leaves of its

X

young branches are like those of the quince, the upper part being green, and the under part whitish and downy; they are the favorite food of the elephants; its fruit consists of small figs of the same size as those of Europe, but not so well tasted; they are of a red colour both within and without. The natives of the country where this tree grows, make some kind of dress of the bark.

"The kasta of the Island of Rodriguez has a leaf the size of a human hand; it is thick, and resembles the shape of an heart, like that of the lilac, and to the touch is soft as satin. The flower is white, and emits a pleasing odour; the fruit is round, its colour red, and of the size of a small plum; its skin is hard, and contains small seeds like those of figs; it is not unwholesome, but its taste is insipid; it is the common food of the bats, who roost in great numbers among the tufted branches of the tree.

"The wood of the trees in this island is, in general, very hard; that which we employed in building our huts became full of worms within a few weeks after it was cut down, but if it is left to soak during a month in the sea, the worm cannot enter it.

There are no four-footed animals at Rodriguez, but rats, lizards, and land turtles. There are sea turtles in great abundance, and some of them have been taken that weighed upwards of a quarter of a ton. They lay their eggs in sandy places, near the sea, and always in the night, they deposit them in a hole about three feet in depth, and a foot broad; having covered them with sand, they leave them to be hatched by the heat, which effects the purpose at the end of six weeks; the young ones, at their birth, are not larger than chickens, and on coming out of the shell, hurry instantly to the sea; we sometimes diverted ourselves with carrying some of them a quarter of a league within land; when, being placed on the ground, they took the straight road to the sea. At this period they walk or crawl faster than when they are grown to a larger size. The frégates (sular fregata) and many other birds destroy them in such numbers that not a tenth part escapes from such voracious enemies.

"The most remarkable bird in this island is the solitaire, so called because it is never seen in flocks. The plumage of the males is gray, intermixed with brown; their feet and beak resemble those of the turkey, though the latter is rather more crooked; they have scarce any tail, and their hinder part is covered with feathers, in such a manner as to give it a round appearance.

"They are taller than the turkey, and have a straight neck, somewhat longer in proportion than that bird, when it erects its head; they have a black and lively eye, but are without crest or top-knot; they never fly, as their wings are not sufficiently strong to sustain the weight of their bodies, and they employ them principally as the means of attack or defence, or to call to one another; for this latter purpose, they turn round twenty or thirty times with great velocity, when their wings, being outspread, the motion produces a noise which resembles that of a kestril, and may be heard at the distance of an hundred yards. The bone of the pinion enlarges at the extremity, and forms, under its feathers, a small round lump like a musket ball, which, with the beak, forms its principal defence. It is very difficult to catch it in the woods, but in an open space it is easily overtaken.

"From March to September these birds are very fat, and, when young, yield a well flavoured meat; the males sometimes weigh between forty and fifty pounds. The hen is a most beautiful bird; some of them are white, and others brown; they have a kind of band, resembling what is called a widow's peak, at the top of the bill, which is of a tan colour; they take great care to keep their feathers in a nice state of arrangement, and to clean themselves with their beak. The feathers that cover the thighs are curled at the end, so as to have the appearance of shells, and, as they are very thick, produce an agreeable effect; they have two projections on the croop, which are formed of feathers whiter than the rest, and curiously represents a bosom.

"These birds walk with so much stateliness and grace as must excite the admiration of all who behold them, and they have often been indebted for their lives to their pleasing appearance. Though they appear rather of a familiar disposition, when they are left to themselves, it is impossible to domesticate them. Whenever they are taken they shed tears without making the least noise, and obstinately refuse all kind of food, so that they soon die for the want of nourishment. Their gizzard is always found to contain a brown stone, of the size of an hen's egg, and of a rugged exterior; it is flat on one side and round on the other, and is very heavy and hard. This stone appears to be born with them, as they are found to contain it when quite young, besides, the channel that passes from the stomach to the gizzard is much too narrow to afford a passage for it.

"We made use of this stone in preference to many others, to sharpen our knives. This bird builds its nest upon an heap of palm leaves, which it raises about a foot and a half from the ground for that purpose. It lays but one egg, which is larger than that of our European goose; the cock and hen both sit on it in their turns, and the time necessary for hatching extends to seven weeks. During the whole period of incubation, and nourishing the nestling, which is not capable of supporting itself for several months after its birth, the parent birds do not suffer any of their kind to approach them; the hen reserving to itself the right of driving away the intrusive females, and the cock exercising his office of guarding the privileged spot against male intruders; each calling the other, as occasion requires, to perform the duty assigned it. When the young bird is in a state to maintain itself, the parents continue their union.

"We often remarked, fabulous as it may

appear, that within a few days after the young one had quitted the nest, a troop of thirty or forty of the old ones brought another of the same age to the spot, where the former, with its parents, joined the troop, and they all proceeded to some retired place, when the elder birds retired in pairs, and left the two young ones to themselves. As we frequently followed them on these occasions, I vouch for the truth of this extraordinary circumstance, which we observed with equal surprise and satisfaction.

"In the Island of Rodriguez there is but one kind of small bird, and it resembles the canary bird; we however never heard it sing, though it was so familiar as to perch on a book at the moment we were reading it.

"There are green and blue paroquets in great abundance, which are of a moderate size; the flesh of the young ones is as delicate as that of young pigeons. There are also sea larks and snipes, and a very few swallows. The bats fly about during the day like other birds; they are as large as a pullet, and each wing is about two feet in length; they never perch, but hook themselves to the branches of trees by their feet, with their head hanging downwards; as their wings are also furnished with hooks, they do not readily fall to the ground when struck, but remain attached to the boughs; indeed, when seen at some distance, enveloped in their wings, they have the appearance of fruit rather than birds. In the Isle of France they are considered as a delicate food, we, however, could not bring ourselves to eat them. They carry their young, of which they have always two, wherever they go, and never quit them until they are able to fly.

"The palm trees and lataniers are covered with lizards, about a foot in length, whose beauty was a frequent object of our admiration; they are black, gray, blue, green, and red, and of the most beautiful tints; their common food is the fruit of the palm tree. They are not in the least obnoxious, and we found them so familiar, that they used to come and eat the melons, not only on the table, but from our hands. They are the prey of birds, and particularly of the bitterns; when we threw them down from the trees with a pole, the latter used to run to the spot, and swallow them up before us, notwithstanding our utmost endeavours to obstruct their voracity.

"There is also a nocturnal lizard, of a

grayish colour, and a very unpleasant shape, it is as thick and as long as a man's arm, and its flesh is not unpalatable, it is fond of the latanier.

"The sea occasionally threw on the shore yellow amber and ambergris; we found a large piece of the latter, of whose name and qualities we were altogether ignorant.* The hurricane, to which this island is subject in the months of January and February, is a most formidable enemy; we twice experienced the horrors of it. This furious wind generally springs up after mild weather, and even after a calm. Its extreme violence lasted during the space of an hour; when we saw several large trees laid prostrate, and our own huts shattered to pieces; the sea was in a most terrible state of agitation, and, raising its billows like mountains, drove them against the shore with such impetuosity that they seemed to threaten its existence. The heavens were confounded with the earth; the air thickened, and covered us with darkness, while the clouds, rolling over each other,

* It is not generally known that this valuable article of commerce is the fæces of the sperm whale, when in a constipated state, occasioned through a disease which that fish is subject to.

Y

dissolved in such streams of rain, that the fine and fertile valleys exhibited a general inundation, where torrents bore down every thing before them. The animals instinctively preserved themselves from the fury of the storm, by taking refuge in the holes of the mountains; they soon however re-appeared, as the weather in a short time re-assumed its serene and pleasant state. The last of the two hurricanes, which we experienced at Rodriguez, was much more terrible than the former; in the midst of its greatest violence there was a sudden calm, and extraordinary stillness, which induced us to suppose that it had passed away, but it soon returned with a renewed and aggravated fury; it entirely destroyed all our gardens, by overwhelming them with a deluge of salt water; but as the soil was not injured by that circumstance, our first occupation, on quitting the recesses of the rocks, where we had taken shelter, was to sow our seeds, as we had already done. The last enemy with which we had to contend was the green caterpillar, which always succeeds the hurricanes. These reptiles greatly annoyed us, from February to April, by eating our melons, of which they would not leave a single leaf. Experience, however, at length taught us to keep the plants covered between sunset and sunrise, by which precaution they were at length preserved; as this vermin did not touch either endive or purslane, it may be reasonably presumed that there are other herbs and vegetables which would be unpalateable to them. There is also small scorpions in some parts of the island, but they are by no means dangerous, as we were stung by them without any other inconvenience than the sensation of being pricked by a pin. When we bathed in the sea, or waded in it for the purpose of fishing, we were often surrounded by shoals of sharks, some of which were of a large size, without receiving the least injury from them. There is every reason to conclude that the sharks of these parts are of a different kind from those which frequent other seas, where they are described and known to be of a most dangerous and ravenous nature.

"Our occupations, during our abode in the island, were not, as it may be imagined, very important, but it was necessary to do something. The repairs of our huts, and the cultivation of our gardens, employed one portion of our time, and walking engaged another; we often went to ths southward of the island, which we crossed in all directions, and sometimes made the tour of it, nor is there a single spot that we have not frequently visited; neither the high mountains, nor the lesser hills are without verdure, though they are very rocky, but there is from two to four feet depth of earth above the rock; at the same time large and strait trees are seen to arise between the crags. There are few or no places in the island which are not easy of access, and in every part there is plenty of provision and water. If no kind of fowl is visible, you have only to strike a tree with force, and hollow aloud, which will occasion them instantly to hasten to it, when they may be easily struck down with a stick or a stone. It was by the following accident that we discovered this singular circumstance. As we were one day rambling about at a distance from each other, it became necessary for us to shout very loud, in order to collect the company, when we were astonished to see the birds flying, and coming from all parts round us, so that a single discharge of our pieces was sufficient to procure us plenty. The land turtle is likewise to be found every where; and the air is so mild and temperate that there is no reason to apprehend any inconvenience from sleeping beneath the canopy of heaven ; shelter however is easily obtained, and a few leaves of latanier may at any time be contrived to afford it. Besides our little journeys, we seldom failed to take our evening walks. One of them possessed so much beauty as to deserve a particular description ; it extended along the sea shore, to the left of the rivulet ; it consisted of a natural avenue of trees, which was as straight as if it had been planted with a line ; it ran parallel with the sea, was about twelve hundred paces in length, and might be continued for seven or eight miles ; one side of this charming spot presented a vast expanse of ocean, whose tide, rolling over the breakers, at a distance of about a league, producing a confused but pleasing murmur ; the other side offered a view of the most delightful valleys, which wore the appearance of beautiful orchards, in the mild and rich season of autumn, and were bounded by a fine range of hills, that closed the prospect. Among the great number and variety of trees which nature has lavished on this spot, there is one which deserves particular attention for its beauty, grandeur, and the symmetrical arrangement of its magnificent branches ; their extremities are tufted in a very extraordinary

manner, while its large an
around, almost on the g
whatever side this fine t
very small part, if any,
ceptible; within its shade
that appear like timber w
trived to support the la
which, spreading aroun
natural pavilion, the fresl
brage is inexpressibly gra

The fruit however is c
taste, not unlike that of
there is no reason to supp
it grows in clusters, and
tance like the fruit of the
The leaves, which are of
short a stalk, that they
to the tree itself, the lar
inches broad at the upper
in a point, their length
inches, while the fruit,
colours, according as it
vanced in maturity, ap
The whole presented an
vegetable grandeur and be

"In this solitary situa
selves with chess, &c. I
from their facilities, did n

of occupations, and to vary our amusements we sometimes did not disdain to instruct the imitative faculties of the parroquets, which are so numerous in this island; during the last year we were often occupied in building the boat, whose history will be given hereafter, and we lengthened out our day by the aid of our lamps, which were supplied with the oil of turtle. We employed burning-glasses to light our fires. As we had flesh and fish in abundance, with herbs, roots, fruit, and palm wine, there was no reason to apprehend any inconvenience from a dearth of provisions; on the contrary, we were nourished with very wholesome, and even luxurious food, which never occasioned the least sickness or indigestion, though we were without bread, the captain had, indeed, left two large barrels of biscuit, which was principally employed in thickening our soup. We had already been more than a year in this island, when we became uneasy that no vessel had arrived there, nor were we free from alarm that a portion of the best part of our lives might be passed in this unprofitable solitude. It was at length resolved among us that after having waited for news from M. du Quesne during two whole years, we should manner, while its large and thick foliage drops around, almost on the ground, so that, on whatever side this fine tree is approached, a very small part, if any, of its trunk is perceptible; within its shade there are branches that appear like timber work, expressly contrived to support the large tuft of foliage, which, spreading around, form a kind of natural pavilion, the freshness of whose umbrage is inexpressibly grateful.

The fruit however is of a sour unpleasant taste, not unlike that of a ripe quince, but there is no reason to suppose it unwholesome; it grows in clusters, and appeared at a distance like the fruit of the unana (pine apple). The leaves, which are of a fine green, have so short a stalk, that they seem to be attached to the tree itself, the largest are four or five inches broad at the upper part, and terminate in a point, their length being about fifteen inches, while the fruit, which is of different colours, according as it is more or less advanced in maturity, appears between them. The whole presented an astonishing object of vegetable grandeur and beauty.

"In this solitary situation we amused ourselves with chess, &c. Hunting and fishing, from their facilities, did not deserve the name of occupations, and to vary our amusements we sometimes did not disdain to instruct the imitative faculties of the parroquets, which are so numerous in this island; during the last year we were often occupied in building the boat, whose history will be given hereafter, and we lengthened out our day by the aid of our lamps, which were supplied with the oil of turtle. We employed burning-glasses to light our fires. As we had flesh and fish in abundance, with herbs, roots, fruit, and palm wine, there was no reason to apprehend any inconvenience from a dearth of provisions; on the contrary, we were nourished with very wholesome, and even luxurious food, which never occasioned the least sickness or indigestion, though we were without bread, the captain had, indeed, left two large barrels of biscuit, which was principally employed in thickening our soup. We had already been more than a year in this island, when we became uneasy that no vessel had arrived there, nor were we free from alarm that a portion of the best part of our lives might be passed in this unprofitable solitude. It was at length resolved among us that after having waited for news from M. du Quesne during two whole years, we should do our utmost to get to the Island of Mauritius, as vessels arrived there every year from the Cape of Good Hope, that island not being more than eighty leagues from Rodriguez, though in our situation it was natural to consider it a very long passage, but as the wind blew regularly on that quarter, it was determined that we should instantly build a boat in the best manner in our power, and if there was any probability of its being capable of service, attempt the voyage. The undertaking appeared to be pregnant with difficulties, but not altogether impracticable, we were, indeed, to construct a large boat, without intelligent workmen, and with few tools, besides, we had neither pitch, tar, ropes, anchor or compass, in short a thousand other obstacles presented themselves to the reflection, and filled us with alarm; it was nevertheless resolved to set about the work, and if we did not lose our labour, to proceed on the voyage, accordingly, without apprenticeship or experience, we in an instant became carpenters, rope-makers, sailors, &c. and proceeded to employ our united efforts to forward the important object we had in view.

"The sea fortunately had thrown upon the shore a large square oak beam, of sixty fee in length, which was sawed into planks, but as the saw broke three times in performing this office, and was also handled with little skill, they were of unequal thickness, and altogether indifferently shaped. Our bark was twenty-two feet long at the keel, six broad, four deep, and round at both ends; we were provided with a small quantity of nails, and Jean de la Haye, the goldsmith, who had some instruments of his trade along with him, forged others, as well as some useful iron tools; he had contrived also to mend the saw; old linen was employed for the purpose of caulking, and a kind of jet, when mixed with the gum of the place, dissolved in turtle oil, served as pitch. We twisted the fibres of the latanier leaves into ropes, which were of sufficient strength, but defective in pliancy, and they frayed also, in a short time, when employed in running work; a piece of rock, which weighed about an hundred and fifty pounds, served for an anchor, and we formed a sail as well as we could; thus, by the joint contribution of our industry, the boat was completed, and, by our united strength launched into the water; for our stock of provisions a sufficient quantity of dried lamentin was prepared, and several barrels were filled with water; we also took the biscuit that remained, and furnished ourselves with plenty both of land and water melons, the latter of which may be kept for a considerable time; we were so fortunate, also, in a general search for whatever might be of use, as to find a small solar quadrant, which, though of a very inferior kind, we flattered ourselves might be useful in our projected expedition; when, however, the boat was launched, we discovered that it did not obey the rudder, and we were under the necessity of supplying its place with an oar. The day fixed for our departure was Saturday the 19th April 1693, because it was near the full moon, when the state of the tide would enable us to pass the breakers, and we should possess light the greater part of the night. These breakers surrounded the island, with the exception of two openings, which gave access to it. When we arrived at Rodriguez, we perceived, on the bark of several trees, the names of certain Dutchmen who had landed there some years before, and had left the date of that circumstance; we accordingly determined to follow their example, and consequently wrote a brief account of our history in French and Flemish, particularly specifying the date of our arrival, the time of our abode, and the day of our departure; this document was inclosed in a phial, which was placed in a niche, cut in the trunk of a large tree, beneath whose shade we used to take our meals, and which we believed to be proof against the violence of the hurricanes. At length the day of our departure arrived, and after having implored divine assistance and protection, of which we appeared to be in great need, we embarked about noon, with our provisions and our property; the weather was fine and the wind favourable, and though the boat was, as may be supposed, of an imperfect construction, and wretchedly equipped, we were animated with the most sanguine hope of succeeding in our expedition. We reckoned indeed, if the fine weather continued, and the kind of monsoon, which has already been mentioned, prevailed, that, according to our calculation, founded on the information of the captain and sailors during our passage, we should arrive in two days and two nights at the Island of Mauritius. We accordingly departed, with the animating hope that we should find ourselves among the inhabitants of the world. The space between the island and the breakers was soon passed, but we relied too much on our good fortune, for, instead of endeavouring to make our way through one of the openings already mentioned, we passed over the breakers, and the boat unfortunately struck one of their points in its passage, but as we scarcely felt any shock, we flattered ourselves that no mischief would ensue; we were however deceived, for a leak soon appeared, and the water gained so rapidly upon us, that we instantly determined to regain the land; in the mean time the boat was filling, the helm was of no use, the wind blew us away, and fear prevented us for some time from employing any means of preservation; at length, however, the love of life instigated us to exertion, and by employing the oars, and having a leading wind, the breakers were soon repassed, but about thirty paces beyond them the boat sank."

Having recovered their boat, they lost one of their companions, Isaac Boyce. After great difficulty in making the boat sea-worthy, they made a second attempt to leave the island, and they ultimately succeeded on the 21st of May, 1693. After a passage full of frightful apprehensions, as to the result, they arrived at the Island of Mauritius, at 5 P.M., on the 29th of May. Immediately after, from the favourable report of these adventurers, a few

Zeitfracht Medien GmbH
Ferdinand-Jühlke-Straße 7
99095 Erfurt, Deutschland
produktsicherheit@kolibri360.de